Matthew Arnold

A French Eton

Or, Middle Class Education and the State

Matthew Arnold

A French Eton
Or, Middle Class Education and the State

ISBN/EAN: 9783337178352

Printed in Europe, USA, Canada, Australia, Japan

Cover: Foto ©ninafisch / pixelio.de

More available books at **www.hansebooks.com**

A

FRENCH ETON;

OR,

MIDDLE CLASS EDUCATION

AND THE STATE.

BY

MATTHEW ARNOLD,

tely Foreign Assistant Commissioner to the Commissioners appointed to inquire into the State of Popular Education in England.

London and Cambridge:
MACMILLAN AND CO.
1864.

A FRENCH ETON;

OR,

MIDDLE-CLASS EDUCATION AND THE STATE.

A LIVELY and acute writer, whom English society, indebted to his vigilance for the exposure of a thousand delinquents, salutes with admiration as its Grand Detective, some time ago called public attention to the state of the "College of the Blessed Mary" at Eton. In that famous seat of learning, he said, a vast sum of money was expended on education, and a beggarly account of empty brains was the result. Rich endowments were wasted; parents were giving large sums to have their children taught, and were getting a most inadequate return for their outlay. Science, among those venerable towers in the vale of the Thames, still adored her Henry's holy shade; but she did very little else. These topics, handled with infinite skill and vivacity, produced a strong effect. Public attention, for a moment, fixed itself upon the state of secondary instruction in England. The great class, which is interested in the improvement of this, imagined that the moment was come for making the first step towards that improvement. The comparatively small class, whose children are educated in the existing public schools, thought that some inquiry into the state of these institutions might do good. A Royal Commission was appointed to report upon the endowments, studies, and management of the nine principal public schools of this country—Eton, Winchester, Westminster, Charterhouse, St. Paul's, Merchant Taylors', Harrow, Rugby, and Shrewsbury.

Eton was really the accused, although eight co-respondents were thus summoned to appear with Eton; and in Eton the investigation now completed will probably produce most reform. The reform of an institution which trains so many of the rulers of this country is, no doubt, a matter of considerable importance. That importance is certainly lessened if it is true, as the *Times* tells us, that the real ruler of our country is "The People," although this potentate does not absolutely transact his own business, but delegates that function to the class which Eton educates. But even those who believe that Mirabeau, when he said, *He who administers, governs*, was a great deal nearer the truth than the *Times*, and to whom, therefore, changes at Eton seem indeed matter of great importance, will hardly be disposed to make those changes very sweeping. If Eton does not teach her pupils profound wisdom, we have Oxenstiern's word for it that the world is governed by very little wisdom. Eton, at any rate, teaches her aristocratic pupils virtues which are among the best virtues of an aristocracy—freedom from affectation, manliness, a high spirit, simplicity. It is to be hoped that she teaches something of these virtues to her other pupils also, who, not of the aristocratic class themselves, enjoy at Eton the benefit of contact with aristocracy. For these other pupils, perhaps, a little more learning as well, a somewhat stronger dose of ideas, might be desirable. Above all, it might be desirable to wean them from the easy habits and profuse notions of expense which Eton generates—habits and notions graceful enough in the lilies of the social field, but inconvenient for its future toilers and spinners. To convey to Eton the knowledge that the wine of Champagne does not water the whole earth, and that

there are incomes which fall below 5,000*l.* a year, would be an act of kindness towards a large class of British parents, full of proper pride, but not opulent. Let us hope that the courageous social reformer who has taken Eton in hand may, at least, reap this reward from his labours. Let us hope he may succeed in somewhat reducing the standard of expense at Eton, and let us pronounce over his offspring the prayer of Ajax:—" O boys, may you be cheaper-
" educated than your father, but in other re-
" spects like him; may you have the same loving
" care for the improvement of the British officer,
" the same terrible eye upon bullies and jobbers,
" the same charming gaiety in your frolics with
" the 'Old Dog Tray;'—but may all these gifts
" be developed at a lesser price!"

But I hope that large class which wants the improvement of secondary instruction in this country—secondary instruction, the great first stage of a liberal education, coming between elementary instruction, the instruction in the mother tongue and in the simplest and indispensable branches of knowledge on the one hand, and superior instruction, the instruction given by universities, the second and finishing stage of a liberal education, on the other—will not imagine that the appointment of a Royal Commission to report on nine existing schools can seriously help it to that which it wants. I hope it will steadily say to the limited class whom the reform of these nine schools (if they need reform) truly concerns—*Tua res agitur.* These nine schools are by their constitution such that they profess to reach but select portions of the multitudes that are claiming secondary instruction; and, whatever they might profess, being nine, they *can* only reach select portions. The exhibition which the Royal Commissioners have given us of these schools is indeed very interesting; I hope it will prove very useful. But, for the champions of the true cause of secondary instruction, for those interested in the thorough improvement of this most important concern, the centre of interest is not there. Before the English mind, always prone to throw itself upon details, has by the interesting Report of the Public School Commissioners been led completely to throw itself upon what, after all, in this great concern of secondary instruction, is only a detail, I wish to show, with all the clearness and insistance I can, where the centre of interest really lies.

I.

To see secondary instruction treated as a matter of national concern, to see any serious attempt to make it both commensurate with the numbers needing it and of good quality, we must cross the Channel. The Royal Commissioners have thought themselves precluded, by the limits of their instructions, from making a thorough inquiry into the system of secondary instruction on the Continent. I regret that they did not trust to the vast importance of the subject for procuring their pardon even if they somewhat extended their scope, and made their survey of foreign secondary instruction exact. This they could have done only by investing qualified persons with the commission to seek, in their name, access to the foreign schools. These institutions must be seen at work, and seen by experienced eyes, for their operation to be properly understood and described. But to see them at work the aid of the public authorities abroad is requisite; and foreign governments, most prompt in giving this aid to accredited emissaries, are by no means disposed to extend it to the chance inquirer.

In 1859 I visited France, authorised by the Royal Commissioners who were then inquiring into the state of popular education in England, to seek, in their name, information respecting the French primary schools. I shall never cease to be grateful for the cordial help afforded to me by the functionaries of the French Government for seeing thoroughly the objects which I came to study. The higher functionaries charged with the supervision of primary instruction have the supervision of secondary instruction also; and their kindness enabled me occasionally to see something of the secondary schools—institutions which strongly attracted my interest, but which the Royal Commissioners had not authorised me to study, and which the French Minister of Public Instruction had not directed his functionaries to show me. I thus saw the Lyceum, or public secondary school, of Toulouse—a good specimen of its class. To make clear to the English reader what this class of institutions is, with a view of enabling him to see, afterwards, what is the problem respecting secondary instruction which we in this country really have to solve, I will describe the Toulouse Lyceum.

Toulouse, the chief city of the great plain of Languedoc, and a place of great antiquity, dignity, and importance, has one of the principal lyceums to be found out of Paris. But the chief town of every French department has its lyceum, and the considerable towns of every department have their communal colleges, as the chief town has its lyceum. These establishments of secondary instruction are attached to academies, local centres of the Department of Public Instruction at Paris, of which there are sixteen in France. The head of an academy is called its "rector," and his chief ministers are called "academy-inspectors." The superintendence of all public instruction (under the general control of the Minister of Public Instruction at Paris) was given by M. Guizot's education-law to the academies; that of primary instruction has been, in great measure, taken away from them and given to the prefects; that of secondary or superior instruction still remains to them. Toulouse is the seat of an academy of the first class, with a jurisdiction extending over eight departments; its rector, when I was there in 1859, was an ex-judge of the Paris Court of Cassation, M. Rocher, a man of about sixty, of great intelligence, courtesy, and knowledge of the world. Ill-health had compelled him to resign his judgeship, and the Minister of Public Instruction, his personal friend, had given him the rectorate of Toulouse, the second in France in point of rank, as a kind of dignified retreat. The position of rector in France much resembles that of one of our heads of houses at Oxford or Cambridge. M. Rocher placed me under the guidance of his academy-inspector, M. Peyrot; and M. Peyrot, after introducing me to the primary inspectors of Toulouse, and enabling me to make arrangements with them for visiting the primary schools of the city and neighbourhood, kindly took me over the lyceum, which is under his immediate supervision.

A French lyceum is an institution founded and maintained by the State, with aid from the department and commune. The communal colleges are founded and maintained by the commune, with aid from the State. The Lyceum of Toulouse is held in large and somewhat gloomy buildings, in the midst of the city; old ecclesiastical buildings have in a number of towns been converted by the Government into public-school premises. We were received by the *proviseur*, M. Seignette. The provisor is the chief functionary—the head master—of a French lyceum; he does not, however, himself teach, but manages the business concerns of the school, administers its finances, and is responsible for its general conduct and discipline; his place is one of the prizes of French secondary instruction, and the provisor, having himself served a long apprenticeship as a teacher, has all the knowledge requisite for superintending his professors. He, like the professors, has gone through the excellent normal school out of which the functionaries of secondary instruction are taken, and has fulfilled stringent conditions of training and examination. Three chaplains—Roman Catholic priests—have the charge of the religious instruction of the lyceum; a Protestant minister, however, is specially appointed to give this instruction to pupils whose parents are of the reformed faith, and these pupils attend, on Sundays, their own Protestant places of worship. The lyceum has from three to four hundred scholars; it receives both boarders and day-scholars. In every lyceum which receives boarders there are a certain number of *bourses*, or public scholarships, which relieve their holders from all cost for their education. The school has three great divisions, each with its separate schoolrooms and playground. The playgrounds are large courts, planted with trees. Attached to the institution, but in a separate building, is a school for little boys from six to twelve years of age, called the *Petit Collège;* here there is a garden as well as a playground, and the whole school-life is easier and softer than in the lyceum, and adapted to the tender years of the scholars. In the *Petit Collège,* too, there are both boarders and day-scholars.

The schoolrooms of the lyceum were much like our schoolrooms here; large bare rooms, looking as if they had seen much service, with their desks browned and battered, and inscribed with the various carvings of many generations of schoolboys. The cleanliness, order, and neatness of the passages, dormitories, and sick-rooms were exemplary. The dormitories are vast rooms, with a teacher's bed at each end; a light is kept burning in them all the night through. In no English school have I seen any arrangements for the sick to compare with those of the Toulouse Lyceum. The service of the *infirmary,* as it is called, is performed by Sisters of Charity. The aspect and manners of these nurses, the freshness and airiness of the rooms, the whiteness and fragrance of the great stores of linen which one saw ranged in them, made one almost envy the invalids who were being tended in such a place of repose.

In the playground the boys—dressed, all of them, in the well-known uniform of the French schoolboy—were running, shouting, and playing, with the animation of their age; but it is not by its playgrounds and means of recreation that a French lyceum, as compared with the half-dozen great English public schools, shines. The boys are taken out to walk, as the boys at Winchester used to be taken out to *hills*; but at the end of the French schoolboy's walk there are no *hills* on which he is turned loose. He learns and practises gymnastics more than our schoolboys do; and the court in which he takes his recreation is somewhat more spacious and agreeable than we English are apt to imagine a *court* to be; but it is a poor place indeed—poor in itself and poor in its resources—compared with the *playing-fields* of Eton, or the *meads* of Winchester, or the *close* of Rugby.

Of course I was very desirous to see the boys in their schoolrooms, and to hear some of the lessons; but M. Peyrot and M. Seignette, with all the good-will in the world, were not able to grant to an unofficial visitor permission to do this. It is something to know what the pro-

A French Eton.

gramme of studies in a French lyceum is, though it would be far more interesting to know how that programme is practically carried out. But the programme itself is worth examining: it is the same for every lyceum in France. It is fixed by the Council of Public Instruction in Paris, a body in which the State, the Church, the French Academy, and the scholastic profession, are all represented, and of which the Minister of Public Instruction is president. The programme thus fixed is promulgated by the Minister's authority, and every lyceum is bound to follow it. I have before me that promulgated by M. Guizot in 1833; the variations from it, up to the present day, are but slight. In the sixth, or lowest class, the boys have to learn French, Latin, and Greek Grammar, and their reading is Cornelius Nepos and Phædrus, and, along with the fables of Phædrus, those of La Fontaine. For the next, or fifth class, the reading is Ovid in Latin, Lucian's Dialogues and Isocrates in Greek, and *Télémaque* in French. For the fourth, besides the authors read in the classes below, Virgil in Latin and Xenophon in Greek, and, in French, Voltaire's *Charles XII.* For the third, Sallust and Cicero are added in Latin, Homer and Plutarch's *Moralia* in Greek; in

French, Voltaire's *Siècle de Louis XIV.*, Massilon's *Petit Carême*, Boileau, and extracts from Buffon. For the second class (our fifth form), Horace, Livy, and Tacitus, in Latin; in Greek, Sophocles and Euripides, Plato and Demosthenes; in French, Bossuet's *Histoire Universelle*, and Montesquieu's *Grandeur et Décadence des Romains*. The highest class (our sixth form) is divided into two, a rhetoric and a philosophy class; this division—which is important, and which is daily becoming, with the authorities of French Public Instruction, an object of greater importance—is meant to correspond to the direction, literary or scientific, which the studies of the now adult scholar are to take. In place of the Pindar, Thucydides, Lucan, and Molière, of the rhetoric class, the philosophy class has chemistry, physics, and the higher mathematics. Some instruction in natural science finds a place in the school-course of every class; in the lower classes, instruction in the elements of human physiology, zoology, botany, and geology; in the second class (fifth form), instruction in the elements of chemistry. To this instruction in natural science two or three hours a week are allotted. About the same time is allotted to arithmetic, to special instruction in history and

A French Eton.

geography, and to modern languages; these last, however, are said to be in general as imperfectly learnt in the French public schools as they are in our own. Two hours a week are devoted to the correction of composition. Finally, the New Testament, in Latin or Greek, forms a part of the daily reading of each class.

On this programme I will make two remarks, suggested by comparing it with that of any of our own public schools. It has the scientific instruction and the study of the mother-tongue which our school-course is without, and is often blamed for being without. I believe that the scientific instruction actually acquired by French schoolboys in the lower classes is very little, but still a boy with a taste for science finds in this instruction an element which keeps his taste alive; in the special class at the head of the school it is more considerable, but not, it is alleged, sufficient for the wants of this special class, and plans for making it more thorough and systematic are being canvassed. In the study of the mother-tongue the French school-boy has a more real advantage over ours; he does certainly learn something of the French language and literature, and of the English our schoolboy learns nothing. French grammar, however, is a better instrument of instruction for boys than English grammar, and the French literature possesses prose works, perhaps even poetical works, more fitted to be used as classics for schoolboys than any which English literature possesses. I need not say that the fitness of works for this purpose depends on other considerations than those of the genius alone, and of the creative force, which they exhibit.

The regular school-lessons of a lyceum occupy about twenty-two hours in the week, but among these regular school-lessons the lessons in modern languages are not counted. The lessons in modern languages are given out of school-hours; out of school-hours, too, all the boarders work with the masters at preparing their lessons; each boarder has thus what we call a private tutor, but the French schoolboy does not, like ours, pay extra for his private tutor: the general charge for board and instruction covers this special tuition.

Now I come to the important matter of school-fees. These are all regulated by authority; the scale of charges in every lyceum and communal college must be seen and sanctioned by the academy-inspector in order to have legality. A day-scholar in the Toulouse Lyceum pays, in the lowest of the three great divisions of the school, 110f. (4*l.* 8*s.* 4*d.*) a year; in the second division he pays 135f. (5*l.* 8*s.* 4*d.*); in the third and highest division, 180f. (7*l.* 4*s.* 2*d.*) If he wishes to share in the special tuition of the boarders, he pays from 2*l.* to 4*l.* a year extra. Next, for the boarders. A boarder pays, for his whole board and instruction, in the lowest division, 800f. (32*l.*) a year; in the second division, 850f. (34*l.*); in the highest division, 900f. (36*l.*) In the scientific class the charge is 2*l.* extra. The payments are made quarterly, and always in advance. Every boarder brings with him an outfit (*trousseau*) valued at 500f. (20*l.*) : the sum paid for his board and instruction covers, besides, all expense for keeping good this outfit, and all charges for washing, medical attendance, books, and writing materials. The meals, though plain, are good, and they are set out with a propriety and a regard for appearances which, when I was a boy, graced no school-dinners that I ever saw; just as, I must say, even in the normal schools for elementary teachers, the dinner-table in France contrasted strongly, by its clean cloth, arranged napkins, glass, and general neatness of service, with the stained cloth, napkinless knives and forks, jacks and mugs, hacked joints of meat, and stumps of loaves, which I have seen on the dinner-table of normal schools in England. With us it is always the individual that is filled, and the public that is sent empty away.

Such may be the cheapness of public school education, when that education is treated as a matter of public economy, to be administered upon a great scale, with rigid system and exact superintendence, in the interest of the pupil and not in the interest of the school-keeper.* But many people, it will be said, have no relish for such cast-iron schooling. Well, then, let us look at a French school not of the State-pattern—a school without the guarantees of State-management, but, also, without the uniformity and constraint which this management introduces.

A day or two after I had seen the Toulouse Lyceum, I started for Sorèze. Sorèze is a village in the department of the Tarn, a department bordering upon that in which Toulouse stands; it contains one of the most successful private

---

* *L'administration des lycées est complètement étrangère a toute idée de spéculation et de profit,* says the Toulouse prospectus which lies before me; "A lyceum is managed not in the least as a matter of speculation or profit;" and this is not a mere advertising puff, for the public is the real proprietor of the lyceums, which it has founded for the education of its youth, and for that object only; the directors of the lyceum are simple servants of the public, employed by the public at fixed salaries.

schools in France, and of this school, in 1859, the celebrated Father Lacordaire was director. I left Toulouse by railway in the middle of the day; in two hours I was at Castelnaudary, an old Visigoth place, on a hill rising out of the great plain of Languedoc, with immense views towards the Pyrenees on one side and the Cevennes on the other. After rambling about the town for an hour, I started for Sorèze in a vehicle exactly like an English coach; I was outside with the driver, and the other places, inside and outside, were occupied by old pupils of the Sorèze school, who were going there for the annual *fête*, the *Speeches*, to take place the next day. They were, most of them, young men from the universities of Toulouse and Montpellier; two or three were settled in Paris, but, happening to be just then at their homes, at Béziers or Narbonne, they had come over like the rest: they seemed a good set, all of them, and their attachment to their old school and master was more according to one's notions of English school-life than French. We had to cross the *Montagne Noire*, an outlier of the Cevennes; the elevation was not great, but the air, even on the 18th of May in Languedoc, was sharp, the vast distance looked grey and chill, and the whole landscape was severe, lonely, and desolate. Sorèze is in the plain on the other side of the *Montagne Noire,* at the foot of gorges running up into the Cevennes; at the head of these gorges are the basins from which the *Canal du Midi*—the great canal uniting the Mediterranean with the Atlantic—is fed. It was seven o'clock when we drove up the street, shaded with large trees, of Sorèze; my fellow-travellers showed me the way to the school, as I was obliged to get away early the next morning, and wanted, therefore, to make my visit that evening. The school occupies the place of an old abbey, founded in 757 by Pepin the Little; for several hundred years the abbey had been in the possession of the Dominicans, when, in Louis the Sixteenth's reign, a school was attached to it. In this school the king took great interest, and himself designed the dress for the scholars. The establishment was saved at the Revolution by the tact of the Dominican who was then at its head; he resumed the lay dress, and returned, in all outward appearance, to the secular life, and his school was allowed to subsist. Under the Restoration it was one of the most famous and most aristocratic schools in France, but it had much declined when Lacordaire, in 1854, took charge of it. I waited in the monastic-looking court (much of the old abbey remains as part of the present building) while my card, with a letter which the Papal Nuncio at Paris, to whom I had been introduced through Sir George Bowyer's kindness, had obtained for me from the Superior of the Dominicans, was taken up to Lacordaire; he sent down word directly that he would see me; I was shown across the court, up an old stone staircase, into a vast corridor; a door in this corridor was thrown open, and in a large bare room, with no carpet or furniture of any kind, except a small table, one or two chairs, a small book-case, a crucifix, and some religious pictures on the walls, Lacordaire, in the dress of his order, white-robed, hooded, and sandalled, sat before me.

The first public appearance of this remarkable man was in the cause of education. The Charter of 1830 had promised liberty of instruction; liberty, that is, for persons outside the official hierarchy of public instruction to open schools. This promise M. Guizot's celebrated school law of 1833 finally performed; but, in the meantime, the authorities of public instruction refused to give effect to it. Lacordaire and M. de Montalembert opened in Paris, on the 7th of May,

1831, an independent free school, of which they themselves were the teachers; it was closed in a day or two by the police, and its youthful conductors were tried before the Court of Peers and fined. This was Lacordaire's first public appearance; twenty-two years later his last sermon in Paris was preached in the same cause; it was a sermon on behalf of the schools of the Christian Brethren. During that space of twenty-two years he had run a conspicuous career, but on another field than that of education; he had become the most renowned preacher in Europe, and he had re-established in France, by his energy, conviction, and patience, the religious orders banished thence since the Revolution. Through this career I cannot now attempt to follow him; with the heart of friendship and the eloquence of genius, M. de Montalembert has recently written its history; but I must point out two characteristics which distinguished him in it, and which created in him the force by which, as an educator, he worked, the force by which he most impressed and commanded the young. One of these was his passion for firm order, for solid government. He called our age an age "which does not know how to obey— "*qui ne sait guère obéir.*" It is easy to see that this is not so absolutely a matter of reproach as Lacordaire made it; in an epoch of transition society may and must say to its governors, "Govern me according to my spirit, if I am to "obey you." One cannot doubt that Lacordaire erred in making absolute devotion to the Church (*malheur a qui trouble l'Église!*) the watch-word of a gifted man in our century; one cannot doubt that he erred in affirming that "the "greatest service to be rendered to Christianity "in our day was to do something for the revival "of the mediæval religious orders." Still, he seized a great truth when he proclaimed the intrinsic weakness and danger of a state of anarchy; above all, when he applied this truth in the moral sphere he was incontrovertible, fruitful for his nation, especially fruitful for the young. He dealt vigorously with himself, and he told others that the first thing for them was to do the same; he placed character above everything else. "One "may have spirit, learning, even genius," he said, "and not *character;* for want of character our "age is the age of miscarriages. Let us form "Christians in our schools, but, first of all, let us "form Christians in our own hearts; the one "great thing is *to have a life of one's own.*"

Allied to this characteristic was his other—his

passion, in an age which seems to think that progress can be achieved only by our herding together and making a noise, for the antique discipline of retirement and silence. His plan of life for himself, when he first took orders, was to go and be a village curé in a remote province in France. M. de Quélen, the Archbishop of Paris, kept him in the capital as chaplain to the Convent of the Visitation; he had not then commenced the *conferences* which made his reputation; he lived perfectly isolated and obscure, and he was never so happy. "It is with delight," he wrote at this time, "that I find my solitude "deepening round me; 'one can do nothing "without solitude,' is my grand maxim. A "man is formed from within, and not from with-"out. To withdraw and be with oneself and "with God, is the greatest strength there can be "in the world." It is impossible not to feel the serenity and sincerity of these words. Twice he refused to edit the *Univers;* he refused a chair in the University of Louvain. In 1836, when his fame filled France, he disappeared for five years, and these years he passed in silence and seclusion at Rome. He came back in 1841 a Dominican monk; again, at Notre Dame, that eloquence, that ineffable *accent,* led his countrymen and foreigners captive; he achieved his cherished purpose of re-establishing in France the religious orders. Then once more he disappeared, and after a short station at Toulouse consigned himself, for the rest of his life, to the labour and obscurity of Sorèze. "One of the "great consolations of my present life," he writes from Sorèze, "is, that I have now God and the "young for my sole companions." The young, with their fresh spirit, as they instinctively feel the presence of a great character, so, too, irresistibly receive an influence from souls which live habitually with God.

Lacordaire received me with great kindness. He was above the middle height, with an excellent countenance; great dignity in his look and bearing, but nothing ascetic; his manners animated, and every gesture and movement showing the orator. He asked me to dine with him the next day, and to see the school festival, the *fête des anciens élèves;* but I could not stop. Then he ordered lights, for it was growing dark, and insisted on showing me all over the place that evening. While we were waiting for lights he asked me much about Oxford; I had already heard from his old pupils that Oxford was a favourite topic with him, and that he held it up to them as a model of everything that was venerable. Lights came, and we went over the establishment; the school then contained nearly three hundred pupils—a great rise since Lacordaire first came in 1854, but not so many as the school has had in old days. It is said that Lacordaire at one time resorted so frequently to expulsion as rather to alarm people.

Sorèze, under his management, chiefly created interest by the sort of competition which it maintained with the lyceums, or State schools. A private school, in France, cannot be opened without giving notice to the public authorities; the consent of these authorities is withheld if the premises of the proposed school are improper, or if its director fails to produce a certificate of probation and a certificate of competency—that is, if he has not served for five years in a secondary school, and passed the authorised public examination for secondary teachers. Finally, the school is always subject to State-inspection, to ascertain that the pupils are properly lodged and fed, and that the teaching contains nothing contrary to public morality and to the laws; and the school may be closed by the public authorities on an inspector's report, duly verified. Still, for an establishment like the Sorèze school, the actual State-interference comes to very little; the Minister has the power of dispensing with the certificate of probation, and holy orders are accepted in the place of the certificate of competency (the examination in the seminary being more difficult than the examination for this latter). In France the State (Machiavel as we English think it), in naming certain matters as the objects of its supervision in private schools, means what it says, and does not go beyond these matters; and, for these matters, the name of a man like Lacordaire serves as a guarantee, and is readily accepted as such.

All the boys at Sorèze are boarders, and a boarder's expenses here exceed by about 8*l.* or 10*l.* a year his expenses at a lyceum. The programme of studies differs little from that of the lyceums, but the military system of these State schools Lacordaire repudiated. Instead of the vast common dormitories of the lyceums, every boy had his little cell to himself; that was, after all, as it seemed to me, the great difference. But immense stress was laid, too, upon physical education, which the lyceums are said too much to neglect. Lacordaire showed me with great satisfaction the stable, with more than twenty horses, and assured me that all the boys were taught to ride. There was the *salle d'escrime*, where they fenced, the armoury full of guns and swords, the shooting gallery, and so on. All this is in our eyes a little fantastic, and does not replace the want of cricket and football in a good field, and of freedom to roam over the country out of school-hours; in France, however, it is a good deal; and then twice a week all the boys used to turn out with Lacordaire upon the mountains, to their great enjoyment as the Sorèze people said, the Father himself being more vigorous than any of them. And the old abbey school has a small park adjoining it, with the mountains rising close behind, and it has beautiful trees in its courts, and by no means the dismal barrack-look of a lyceum. Lacordaire had a staff of more than fifty teachers and helpers, about half of these being members of his own religious order—Dominicans; all co-operated in some way or other in conducting the school. Lacordaire used never to give school-lessons himself, but scarcely a Sunday passed without his preaching in the chapel. The highest and most distinguished boys formed a body called *the Institute*, with no governing powers like those of our sixth form, but with a sort of common-room to themselves, and with the privilege of having their meals with Lacordaire and his staff. I was shown, too, a *Salle d'Illustres*, or Hall of Worthies, into which the boys are introduced on high days and holidays; we should think this fanciful, but I found it impressive. The hall is decorated with busts of the chief of the former scholars, some of them very distinguished. Among these busts was that of Henri de Larochejacquelin (who was brought up here at Sorèze), with his noble, speaking countenance, his Vendean hat, and the heart and cross on his breast. There was, besides, a theatre for public recitations. We ended with the chapel, in which we found all the school assembled; a Dominican was reading to them from the pulpit an edifying life of a scapegrace converted to seriousness by a bad accident, much better worth listening to than most sermons. When it was over, Lacordaire whispered to me to ask if I would stay for the prayers or go at once. I stayed; they were very short and simple; and I saw the boys disperse afterwards. The gaiety of the little ones and their evident fondness for the *Père* was a pretty sight. As we went out of chapel, one of them, a little fellow of ten or eleven, ran from behind us, snatched, with a laughing face, Lacordaire's hand, and kissed it; Lacordaire smiled, and patted his head. When I read the other day in M. de Montalembert's book how Lacordaire had said, shortly before his death, "I have always tried to serve God, the Church, "and our Lord Jesus Christ; besides these, I "have loved—oh, dearly loved!—children and "young people," I thought of this incident.

Lacordaire knew absolutely nothing of our great English schools, their character, or recent history; but then no Frenchman, except a very few at Paris who know more than anybody in the world, knows anything about anything. However, I have seen few people more impressive; he was not a great modern thinker, but a great Christian orator of the fourth century, born in the nineteenth; playing his part in the nineteenth century not so successfully as he would have played it in the fourth, but still nobly. I would have given much to stay longer with him, as he kindly pressed me; I was tempted, too, by hearing that it was likely he would make a speech the next day. Never did any man so give one the sense of his being a natural orator, perfect in ease and simplicity; they told me that on Sunday, when he preached, he hardly ever went up into the pulpit, but spoke to them from his place "*sans façon.*" But I had an engagement to keep at Carcassone at a certain hour, and I was obliged to go. At nine I took leave of Lacordaire and returned to the village inn, clean, because it is frequented by the relations of pupils. There I supped with my fellow-travellers, the old scholars; charming companions they proved themselves. Late we sat, much *vin de Cahors* we drank, and great friends we became. Before we parted, one of them, the Béziers youth studying at Paris, with the amiability of his race assured me (God forgive him!) that he was well acquainted with my poems. By five the next morning I had started to return to Castelnaudary. Recrossing the *Montagne Noire* in the early morning was very cold work, but the view was inconceivably grand. I caught the train at Castelnaudary, and was at Carcassone by eleven; there I saw a school, and I saw the old *city* of Carcassone. I am not going to describe either the one or the other, but I cannot forbear saying, Let everybody see the *cité de Carcassone.* It is, indeed, as the antiquarians call it, the Middle Age Herculaneum.

When you first get sight of the old city, which is behind the modern town—when you have got clear of the modern town, and come out upon the bridge over the Aude, and see the walled *cité* upon its hill before you—you rub your eyes and think that you are looking at a vignette in *Ivanhoe*.

Thus I have enabled, as far as I could, the English reader to see what a French lyceum is like, and what a French private school, competing with a lyceum, is like. I have given him, as far as I could, the facts; now for the application of these facts. What is the problem respecting secondary instruction which we in this country have to solve? What light do these facts throw upon that problem?

II.

For the serious thinker, for the real student of the question of secondary instruction, the problem respecting secondary instruction which we in England have to solve is this:—Why cannot we have throughout England—as the French have throughout France, as the Germans have throughout Germany, as the Swiss have throughout Switzerland, as the Dutch have throughout Holland—schools where the children of our middle and professional classes may obtain, at the rate of from 20*l.* to 50*l.* a year, if they are boarders, at the rate of from 5*l.* to 15*l.* a year if they are day-scholars, an education of as good quality, with as good guarantees, social character, and advantages for a future career in the world, as the education which French children of the corresponding class can obtain from institutions like that of Toulouse or Sorèze?

There is the really important question. It is vain to meet it by propositions which may, very likely, be true, but which are quite irrelevant. "Your French Etons," I am told, "are no Etons "at all; there is nothing like an Eton in France."

I know that. Very likely France is to be pitied for having no Etons, but I want to call attention to the substitute, to the compensation. The English public school produces the finest boys in the world; the Toulouse Lyceum boy, the Sorèze College boy, is not to be compared with them. Well, let me grant all that too. But then there are only some five or six schools in England to produce this specimen-boy; and they cannot produce him cheap. Rugby and Winchester produce him at about 120*l.* a year; Eton and Harrow (and the Eton school-boy is perhaps justly taken as the most perfect type of this highly-extolled class) cannot produce him for much less than 200*l.* a year. *Tantæ molis erat Romanam condere gentem*—such a business is it to produce an article so superior. But for the common wear and tear of middling life, and at rates tolerable for middling people, what do we produce? What do we produce at 30*l.* a year? What is the character of the schools which undertake for us this humbler, but far more widely-interesting production? Are they as good as the Toulouse Lyceum and the Sorèze College? That is the question.

Suppose that the recommendations of the Public School Commissioners bring about in the great public schools all the reforms which a judicious reformer could desire;—suppose that they produce the best possible application of endowments, the best possible mode of election to masterships; that they lead to a wise revision of the books and subjects of study, to a reinforcing of the mathematics and of the modern languages, where these are found weak; to a perfecting, finally, of all boarding arrangements and discipline: nothing will yet have been done towards providing for the great want—the want of a secondary instruction at once reasonably cheap and reasonably good. Suppose that the recommendations of the Commissioners accomplish something even in this direction—suppose that the cost of educating a boy at Rugby is reduced to about 100*l.* a year, and the cost of educating a boy at Eton to about 150*l.* a year— no one acquainted with the subject will think it practicable, or even, under present circumstances, desirable, to effect in the cost of education in these two schools a greater reduction than this. And what will this reduction amount to? A boon—in some cases a very considerable boon— to those who now frequent these schools. But what will it do for the great class now in want of proper secondary instruction? Nothing: for in the first place these schools are but two, and are full, or at least sufficiently full, already; in the second place, if they were able to hold all the boys in England, the class I speak of would still be excluded from them—excluded by a cost of 100*l.* or 150*l.* just as much as by a cost of 120*l.* or 200*l.* A certain number of the professional class, with incomes quite inadequate to such a charge, will, for the sake of the future establishment of their children, make a brave effort, and send them to Eton or Rugby at a cost of 150*l.* or 100*l.* a year. But they send them there already, even at the existing higher rate. The great mass of middling people, with middling incomes, not having for their children's future establishment in life plans which make a public school training indispensable, will not make this effort, will not pay for their children's schooling a price quite disproportionate to their means. They demand a lower school charge—a school-charge like that of Toulouse or Sorèze.

And they find it. They have only to open the *Times*. There they read advertisement upon advertisement, offering them, "conscientiously "offering" them, in almost any part of England which suits their convenience, " Education, 20*l.* " per annum, no extras. Diet unlimited, and

"of the best description. The education com-
"prises Greek, Latin, and German, French by a
"resident native, mathematics, algebra, mapping,
"globes, and all the essentials of a first-rate
"commercial education." Physical, moral, mental,
and spiritual—all the wants of their children
will be sedulously cared for. They are invited
to an "Educational Home," where "discipline is
"based upon moral influence and emulation, and
"every effort is made to combine home-comforts
"with school-training. Terms inclusive and mo-
"derate." If they have a child with an awkward
temper, and needing special management, even
for this particular child the wonderful operation
of the laws of supply and demand, in this great
commercial country, will be found to have made
perfect provision. "Unmanageable boys or youths
"(up to twenty years) are made perfectly tract-
"able and gentlemanly in one year by a clergy-
"man near town, whose peculiarly persuasive high
"moral and religious training at once elevates,"
&c. And all this, as I have said, is provided
by the simple, natural operation of the laws of
supply and demand, without, as the *Times* beau-
tifully says, "the fetters of endowment and the
"interference of the executive." Happy country!
happy middle classes! Well may the *Times*

congratulate them with such fervency; well may it produce dithyrambs, while the newspapers of less-favoured countries produce only leading articles; well may it declare that the fabled life of the Happy Islands is already beginning amongst us.

But I have no heart for satire, though the occasion invites it. No one, who knows anything of the subject, will venture to affirm that these "educational homes" give, or can give, that which they "conscientiously offer." No one, who knows anything of the subject, will seriously affirm that they give, or can give, an education comparable to that given by the Toulouse and Sorèze schools. And why? Because they want the securities which, to make them produce even half of what they offer, are indispensable—the securities of supervision and publicity. By this time we know pretty well that to trust to the principle of supply and demand to do for us all that we want in providing education is to lean upon a broken reed. We trusted to it to give us fit elementary schools till its impotence became conspicuous; we have thrown it aside, and called upon State-aid, with the securities accompanying this, to give us elementary schools more like what they should be; we have thus founded in elementary education a system still, indeed, far from perfect, but living and fruitful —a system which will probably survive the most strenuous efforts for its destruction. In secondary education the impotence of this principle of supply and demand is as signal as in elementary education. The mass of mankind know good butter from bad, and tainted meat from fresh, and the principle of supply and demand may, perhaps, be relied on to give us sound meat and butter. But the mass of mankind do not so well know what distinguishes good teaching and training from bad; they do not here know what they ought to demand, and, therefore, the demand cannot be relied on to give us the right supply. Even if they knew what they ought to demand, they have no sufficient means of testing whether or no this is really supplied to them. Securities, therefore, are needed. The great public schools of England offer securities by their very publicity; by their wealth, importance, and connexions, which attract general attention to them; by their old reputation, which they cannot forfeit without disgrace and danger. The appointment of the Public School Commission is a proof, that to these moral securities for the efficiency of the great public schools may be added the material security of occasional competent supervision. I will grant that the great schools of the Continent do not offer the same moral securities to the public as Eton or Harrow. They offer them in a certain measure, but certainly not in so large measure: they have not by any means so much importance, by any means so much reputation. Therefore they offer, in far larger measure, the other security—the security of competent supervision. With them this supervision is not occasional and extraordinary, but periodic and regular; it is not explorative only; it is also, to a considerable extent, authoritative.

It will be said that between the "educational home" and Eton there is a long series of schools, with many gradations; and that in this series are to be found schools far less expensive than Eton, yet offering moral securities as Eton offers them, and as the "educational home" does not. Cheltenham, Bradfield, Marlborough, are instances which will occur to every one. It is true that these schools offer securities; it is true that the mere presence, at the head of a school, of a distinguished master like Mr. Bradley is, perhaps, the best moral security which can be offered. But, in the first place, these schools are thinly scattered over the country; we have no provision for planting such schools where they are most wanted, or for insuring a due supply of them. Cheltenham, Bradfield, and Marlborough are no more a due provision for the Northumberland boy than the Bordeaux Lyceum is a due provision for the little Alsatian. In the second place, Are these schools cheap? Even if they were cheap once, does not their very excellence, in a country where schools at once good and cheap are rare, tend to deprive them of their cheapness? Marlborough was, I believe—perhaps it still is—the cheapest of them; Marlborough is probably just now the best-taught school in England; and Marlborough, therefore, has raised its school-charge. Marlborough was quite right in so doing, for Marlborough is an individual institution, bound to guard its own interests and to profit by its own successes, and not bound to provide for the general educational wants of the country. But what makes the school-charge of the Toulouse Lyceum remain moderate, however eminent may be the merits of the Toulouse masters, or the successes of the Toulouse pupils? It is that the Toulouse Lyceum is a public institution, administered in view of the general educational wants of France, and not of its own individual preponderance. And what makes (or made, alas!) the school-charge of the Sorèze College remain moderate, even with a most distinguished and attractive director, like Lacordaire, at its head? It was the organisation of a complete system of secondary schools throughout France, the abundant supply of institutions, with at once respectable guarantees and reasonable charges, fixing a general mean of school-cost which even the most successful private school cannot venture much to exceed.

After all, it is the "educational home," and not Bradfield or Marlborough, which supplies us with the nearest approach to that rate of charges which secondary instruction, if it is ever to be organised on a great scale, and to reach those who are in need of it, must inevitably adopt. People talk of the greater cheapness of foreign countries, and of the dearness of this; everything costs more here, they say, than it does abroad; good education, like everything else. I do not wish to dispute, I am willing to make some allowance for this plea; one must be careful not to make too much, however, or we shall find ourselves to the end of the chapter with a secondary instruction failing just where our present secondary instruction fails—a secondary instruction which, out of the multitude needing it, a few, and only a few, make sacrifices to get; the many, who do not like sacrifices, go without it. If we fix a school-charge varying from 25*l.* to 50*l.* a year, I am sure we have fixed the outside rate which the great body of those needing secondary instruction will ever pay. Sir John Coleridge analyses this body into "the " clergy of moderate or contracted incomes" (and that means the immense majority of the clergy), " officers of the army and navy, medical men, " solicitors, and gentry of large families and small " means." Many more elements might be enumerated. Why are the manufacturers left out? The very rich, among these, are to be counted by ones, the middling sort by hundreds. And when Sir John Coleridge separates " tenant- " farmers, small landholders, and retail trades- " men," into a class by themselves, and proposes to appropriate a separate class of schools for them, he carries the process of distinction and demarcation further than I can think quite desirable. But taking the constituent parts of the class requiring a liberal education as he assigns them, it seems to me certain that a sum ranging from 25*l.* to 50*l.* a year is as much as those whom he enumerates can in general be expected to pay for a son's education, and as much as they need be called upon to pay for a sound and valuable education, if secondary instruction were organised as it might be. It must be remembered, however, that a reduced rate of charge for boarders, at a good boarding-school, is not by any means the only benefit to the class of parents in question—perhaps not even the principal benefit—which the organisation of secondary instruction brings with it. It brings with it, also, by establishing its schools in proper numbers, and all over the country, facilities for bringing up many boys as day-scholars who are now brought up as boarders. At present many people send their sons to a boarding-school when they would much rather keep them at home, because they have no suitable school within reach. Opinions differ as to whether it is best for a boy to live at home or to go away to school, but there can be no doubt which of the two modes of bringing him up is the cheapest for his parents; and those (and they are many) who think that the continuation of home-life along with his schooling is far best for the boy himself, would enjoy a double benefit in having suitable schools made accessible to them.

But I must not forget that an institution, or

rather a group of institutions, exists, offering to the middle classes, at a charge scarcely higher than that of the 20*l.* "educational home," an education affording considerable guarantees for its sound character. I mean the College of St. Nicholas, Lancing, and its affiliated schools. This institution certainly demands a word of notice here, and no word of mine, regarding Mr. Woodard and his labours, shall be wanting in unfeigned interest and respect for them. Still, I must confess that, as I read Mr. Woodard's programme, and as I listened to an excellent sermon from the Dean of Chichester in recommendation of it, that programme and that sermon seemed to me irresistibly to lead towards conclusions which they did not reach, and the conclusions which they did reach were far from satisfying. Mr. Woodard says with great truth: " It may be " asked, Why cannot the shopkeeper-class " educate their own children without charity ? " It may be answered, Scarcely any class in the " country does educate its own children without " some aid. Witness the enormous endowments " of our Universities and public schools, where " the sons of our well-to-do people resort. Witness " our national schools supported by State grants, " and by parochial and national subscriptions.

"On the other hand, the lower middle class" (Mr. Woodard might quite properly have said the middle class in general), "politically a very "important one, is dependent to a great extent " for its education on private desultory enterprise. " This class, in this land of education, gets *nothing* "out of the millions given annually for this " purpose to every class except themselves." In his sermon Dr. Hook spoke, in his cordial, manly way, much to the same effect.

This was the grievance; what was the remedy? That this great class should be rescued from the tender mercies of private desultory enterprise ? That, in this land of education, it should henceforth get something out of the millions given annually for this purpose to every class except itself? That in an age when "enormous endow-"ments,"—the form which public aid took in earlier ages, and taking which form public aid founded in those ages the Universities and the public schools for the benefit, along with the upper class, of this very middle class which is now, by the irresistible course of events, in great measure excluded from them—that in an age, I say, when these great endowments, this mediæval form of public aid, have ceased, public aid should be brought to these classes in that simpler and more manageable form which in modern societies it assumes—the form of public grants, with the guarantees of supervision and responsibility? The Universities receive public grants; for—not to speak of the payment of certain professors* by the State—that the State regards the endowments of the Universities as in reality public grants, it proves by assuming to itself the right of interfering in the disposal of them; the elementary schools receive public grants. Why, then, should not our secondary schools receive public grants? But this question Mr. Woodard (I do not blame him for it, he had a special function to perform) never touches. He falls back on an Englishman's favourite panacea—a subscription. He has built a school at Lancing, and a school at Shoreham, and he proposes to build a bigger school than either at Balcombe. He asks for a certain number of subscribers to give him contributions for a certain number of years, at certain rates, which he has calculated. I cannot see how, in this way, he will be delivering English secondary instruction from the hands

* These professors are now nominally paid by the University; but the University pays them in consideration of the remission to her, by the State, of certain duties of greater amount than the salaries which the State used to pay to these professors. They are still, therefore, in fact, paid by the State.

of "private desultory enterprise." What English secondary instruction wants is these two things ; sufficiency of provision of fit schools, sufficiency of securities for their fitness. Mr. Woodard proposes to establish one great school in Sussex, where he has got two already. What sort of a provision is this for that need which is, on his own showing, so urgent? He hopes, indeed, that "if the public will assist in raising this one "school, it will lead to a general extension of "middle class education all over England." But in what number of years? How long are we to wait first? And then we have to consider the second great point—that of *securities*. Suppose Mr. Woodard's hopes to be fulfilled—suppose the establishment of the Balcombe school to have led to the establishment of like schools all over England—what securities shall we have for the fitness of these schools? Sussex is not a very large and populous county, but, even if we limit ourselves to the ratio adopted for Sussex, of three of these schools to a county, that gives us 120 of them for England proper only, without taking in Wales. I have said that the eminence of the master may be in itself a sound security for the worth of a school; but, when I look at the number of these schools wanted, when I look at the probable position and emoluments of their teachers, I cannot think it reasonable to expect that all of them, or anything like all, will be provided with masters of an eminence to make all further guarantees unnecessary. But, perhaps, they will all be affiliated to the present institution at Lancing, and, in some degree, under its supervision? Well, then, that gives us, as the main regulative power of English secondary instruction, as our principal security for it, the Provost and Fellows of St. Nicholas College, Lancing. I have the greatest, the most sincere respect for Mr. Woodard and his coadjutors—I should be quite ready to accept Mr. Woodard's name as sufficient security for any school which he himself conducts—but I should hesitate, I confess, before accepting Mr. Woodard and his colleagues, or any similar body of private persons, as my final security for the right management of a great national concern, as the last court of appeal to which the interests of English secondary instruction were to be carried. Their constitution is too close, their composition too little national. Even if this or that individual were content to take them as his security, the bulk of the public would not. We saw this the other day, when imputations were thrown out against Lancing, and our proposed security had to find security for itself. It had no difficulty in so doing; Mr. Woodard has, it cannot be repeated too often, governed Lancing admirably; all I mean is—and Mr. Woodard himself would probably be the first to agree with me—that, to command public confidence for a great national system of schools, one needs a security larger, ampler, more national, than any which, by the very nature of things, Mr. Woodard and his friends can quite supply.

But another and a very plausible security has been provided for secondary instruction by the zeal and energy of Mr. Acland and Dr. Temple; I mean, the Oxford and Cambridge Middle Class Examinations. The good intentions and the activity of the promoters of these examinations cannot be acknowledged too gratefully; good has certainly been accomplished by them: yet it is undeniable that this security also is, in its present condition, quite insufficient. I write, not for the professed and practised educationist, but for the general reader; above all, for the reader of that class which is most concerned in the question which I am raising, and which I am most solicitous to carry with me—the middle class. Therefore, I shall use the plainest and most unprofessional language I can, in attempting to show what the promoters of these University examinations try to do, what they have accomplished, wherein they have failed. (They try to make *security* do for us all that we want in the improvement of our secondary education.) They accept the " educational homes " at present scattered all over the country; they do not aim at replacing them by other and better institutions; they do not visit or criticise them ; but they invite them to send select pupils to certain local centres, and when the pupils are there, they examine them, class them, and give prizes to the best of them. Undoubtedly this action of the Universities has given a certain amount of stimulus to these schools, and has done them a certain amount of good. But any one can see how far this action falls, and must fall, short of what is required. Any one can see that the examination of a few select scholars from a school, not at the school itself, not preceded or followed by an inspection of the school itself, affords no solid security for the good condition of their school. Any one can see that it is for the interest of an unscrupulous master to give all his care to his few cleverest pupils, who will serve him as an advertisement, while he neglects the common bulk of his pupils, whose backwardness there will be nobody to expose. I will not, however, insist too strongly on this last mischief, because I really believe that, serious as is its danger, it has not so much prevailed as to counterbalance the benefit which the mere stimulus of these examinations has given. All I say is, that this stimulus is an insufficient security. Plans are now broached for reinforcing University examination by University inspection. There we get a far more solid security. And I agree with Sir John Coleridge, that a body fitter than the Universities to exercise this inspection could not be found. It is indispensable that it should be exercised in the name, and on the responsibility, of a great public body; therefore the Society of Arts, which deserves thanks for its readiness to help in improving secondary instruction, is hardly, perhaps, from its want of weight, authority, and importance, qualified to exercise it: but whether it is exercised by the State, or by great and august corporations like Oxford and Cambridge, the value of the security is equally good; and learned corporations, like the Universities, have a certain natural fitness for discharging what is, in many respects, a learned function. It is only as to the power of the Universities to organise, equip, and keep working an efficient system of inspection for secondary schools that I am in doubt; organisation and regularity are as indispensable to this guarantee as weight and authority. Can the Universities organise and pay a body of inspectors to travel all over England, to visit, at least once in every year, the four or five hundred endowed schools of this country, and its unnumbered "educational homes;" can they supply a machinery for regulating the action of these gentlemen, giving effect to the information received from them, printing their reports, circulating them through the country? The French University could; but the French University was a department of State. If the English Universities cannot, the security of their inspection will be precarious; if they can, there can be no better.

No better *security*. But English secondary instruction wants, I said, two things:—sufficient provision of good schools; sufficient security for these schools continuing good. Granting that the Universities may give us the second, I do not see how they are to give us the first. It is not enough merely to provide a staff of inspectors and examiners, and still to leave the children of our middle class scattered about through the numberless obscure endowed schools and "edu-"cational homes" of this country, some of them good,* many of them middling, most of them bad; but none of them great institutions, none of them invested with much consideration or dignity. What is wanted for the English middle class is *respected* schools, as well as *inspected* ones. I will explain what I mean.

The education of each class in society has, or ought to have, its ideal, determined by the wants of that class, and by its destination. Society may be imagined so uniform that one education shall be suitable for all its members; we have not a society of that kind, nor has any European country. We have to regard the condition of classes, in dealing with education;

---

* A friendly critic, in the *Museum*, complains that my censure of private schools is too sweeping, that I set them all down, all without exception, as utterly bad;—he will allow me to point to these words as my answer. No doubt there are some masters or cheap private schools who are doing honest and excellent work; but no one suffers more than such men themselves do from a state of things in which, from the badness of the majority of these schools, a discredit is cast over them all, bad and good alike; no one would gain more by obtaining a public, trustworthy discrimination of bad from good, an authentic recognition of merit. The teachers of these schools would then have, in their profession, a career; at present they have none.

but it is right to take into account not their immediate condition only, but their wants, their destination—above all, their evident pressing wants, their evident proximate destination. Looking at English society at this moment, one may say that the ideal for the education of each of its classes to follow, the aim which the education of each should particularly endeavour to reach, is different. Mr. Hawtrey, whose admirable and fruitful labours at St. Mark's School entitle him to be heard with great respect, lays it down as an absolute proposition that the *family is the type of the school.* I do not think that is true for the schools of all classes alike. I feel sure my father, whose authority Mr. Hawtrey claims for this maxim, would not have laid it down in this absolute way. For the wants of the highest class—of the class which frequents Eton, for instance—not *school a family*, but rather *school a little world*, is the right ideal. I cannot concede to Mr. Hawtrey that, for the young gentlemen who go to Eton, our grand aim and aspiration should be, in his own words, "to make their boyhood a joyous " one, by gentle usage and friendly confidence " on the part of the master." Let him believe me, the great want for the children of luxury is not this sedulous tenderness, this smoothing of the rose-leaf for them; I am sure that, in fact, it is not by the predominance of the family and parental relation in its school-life that Eton is strongest: and it is well that this is so. It seems to me that, for the class frequenting Eton, the grand aim of education should be to give them those good things which their birth and rearing are least likely to give them: to give them (besides mere book-learning) the notion of a sort of republican fellowship, the practice of a plain life in common, the habit of self-help. To the middle class, the grand aim of education should be to give largeness of soul and personal dignity; to the lower class, feeling, gentleness, humanity. Here, at last, Mr. Hawtrey's ideal of the *family* as the type for the school, comes in its due place; for the children of poverty it is right, it is needful to set oneself first to "make their boyhood a joyous one, by gentle "usage and friendly confidence on the part of "the master;" for them the great danger is not insolence from over-cherishing, but insensibility from over-neglect. Mr. Hawtrey's labours at St. Mark's have been excellent and fruitful, just because he has here applied his maxim where it was the right maxim to apply. Yet even in this sphere Mr. Hawtrey's maxim must not be used too absolutely or too long. Human dignity needs almost as much care as human sensibility. First, undoubtedly, you must make men feeling; but the moment you have done that, you must lose no time in making them magnanimous. Mr. Hawtrey will forgive me for saying that perhaps his danger lies in pressing the spring of gentleness, of confidence, of child-like docility, of "kindly feeling of the dependent towards the "patron who is furthering his well-being" a little too hard. The energy and manliness, which he values as much as any one, run perhaps some little risk of etiolating. At least, I think I can see some indications of this danger in the reports —pleasing as in most respects they are—of his boys' career in the world after they have left school. He does so much for them at St. Mark's, that he brings them to the point at which the ideal of education changes, and the prime want for their culture becomes identical with the prime want for the culture of the middle classes. Their fibre has been suppled long enough; now it wants fortifying.

To do Eton justice, she does not follow Mr. Hawtrey's ideal; she does not supple the fibre of her pupils too much ; and, to do the parents of these pupils justice, they have in general a wholesome sense of what their sons do really most want, and are not by any means anxious that school should over-foster them. But I am afraid our middle classes have not quite to the same degree this just perception of the true wants of their offspring. They wish them to be comfortable at school, to be sufficiently instructed there, and not to cost much. Hence the eager promise of "home comforts" with school teaching, all on "terms inclusive and "moderate," from the conscientious proprietor of the educational home. To be sure, they do not get what they wish. So long as human nature remains what it is, they never will get it, until they take some better security for it than a prospectus. But suppose they get the security of inspection exercised by the Universities, or by any other trustworthy authority. Some good such an inspection would undoubtedly accomplish; certain glaring specimens of charlatanism it might probably expose, certain gross cases of mishandling and neglect it might put a stop to. It might do a good deal for the school teaching, and something for the home comforts. It can never make these last what the prospectuses promise, what the parents who believe the pro-

spectuses hope for, what they might even really
have for their money; for only secondary instruction organised on a great and regular scale
can give this at such cheap cost, and so to
organise secondary instruction the inspection we
are supposing has no power. But even if it had
the power, if secondary instruction were organised
on a great and regular scale, if it were a national
concern, it would not be by ensuring to the offspring of the middle classes a more solid teaching at school, and a larger share of home comforts than they at present enjoy there (though
certainly it would do this), that such a secondary
instruction would confer upon them the greatest
boon. Its greatest boon to the offspring of these
classes would be its giving them great, honourable, public institutions for their nurture—institutions conveying to the spirit, at the time of
life when the spirit is most penetrable, the salu-
tary influences of greatness, honour, and nation-
ality—influences which expand the soul, liberalise
the mind, dignify the character.

Such institutions are the great public schools
of England and the great Universities; with
these influences, and some others to which I
just now pointed, they have formed the upper
class of this country—a class with many faults,

with many shortcomings, but imbued, on the whole, and mainly through these influences, with a high, magnanimous, governing spirit, which has long enabled them to rule, not ignobly, this great country, and which will still enable them to rule it until they are equalled or surpassed. These institutions had their origin in endowments; and the age of endowments is gone. Beautiful and venerable as are many of the aspects under which it presents itself, this form of public establishment of education, with its limitations, its preferences, its ecclesiastical character, its inflexibility, its inevitable want of foresight, proved, as time rolled on, to be subject to many inconveniences, to many abuses. On the Continent of Europe a clean sweep has in general been made of this old form of establishment, and new institutions have arisen upon its ruins. In England we have kept our great school and college foundations, introducing into their system what correctives and palliatives were absolutely necessary. Long may we so keep them! but no such palliatives or correctives will ever make the public establishment of education which sufficed for earlier ages suffice for this, nor persuade the stream of endowment, long since failing and scanty, to flow again for our present needs as it flowed in the middle ages. For public establishments modern societies have to betake themselves to the State ; that is, to *themselves in their collective and corporate character.* On the Continent, society has thus betaken itself to the State for the establishment of education. The result has been the formation of institutions like the Lyceum of Toulouse ; institutions capable of great improvement, by no means to be extolled absolutely, by no means to be imitated just as they are ; but institutions formed by modern society, with modern modes of operation, to meet modern wants ; and in some important respects, at any rate, meeting those wants. These institutions give to a whole new class— to the middle class taken at its very widest— not merely an education for whose teaching and boarding there is valid security, but something— not so much I admit, but something—of the same enlarging, liberalising sense, the sense of belonging to a great and honourable public institution, which Eton and our three or four great public schools give to our upper class only, and to a small fragment broken off from the top of our middle class. That is where England is weak, and France, Holland, and Germany are strong. Education is and must be a matter of public establishment. Other countries have replaced the defective public establishment made by the middle ages for their education with a new one, which provides for the actual condition of things. We in England keep our old public establishment for education. That is very well; but then we must not forget to supplement it where it falls short. We must not neglect to provide for the actual condition of things.

I have no pet scheme to press, no crotchet to gratify, no fanatical zeal for giving this or that particular shape to the public establishment of our secondary instruction. All I say is, that it is most urgent to give to the establishment of it a wider, a truly public character, and that only the State can give this. If the matter is but once fairly taken in hand, and by competent agency, I am satisfied. In this country we do not move fast; we do not organise great wholes all in a day. But if the State only granted for secondary instruction the sum which it originally granted for primary—20,000*l.* a year—and employed this sum in founding scholarships for secondary schools, with the stipulation that all the schools which sent pupils to compete for these scholarships should admit inspection, a beginning would have been made; a beginning

A French Eton.

which I truly believe would, at the end of ten years' time, be found to have raised the character of secondary instruction all through England. If more than this can be attempted at first, Sir John Coleridge, in his two excellent letters on this subject to the *Guardian*, perfectly indicates the right course to take: indeed, one could wish nothing better than to commit the settlement of this matter to men of such prudence, moderation, intelligence, and public character as Sir John Coleridge. The four or five hundred endowed schools, whose collective operations now give so little result, should be turned to better account; amalgamation should be used, the most useful of these institutions strengthened, the most useless suppressed, the whole body of them be treated as one whole, destined harmoniously to co-operate towards one end. What should be had in view is to constitute, in every county, at least one great centre of secondary instruction, with low charges, with the security of inspection, and with a public character. These institutions should bear some such title as that of *Royal Schools*, and should derive their support, mainly, of course, from school-fees, but partly, also, from endowments—their own, or those appropriated to them—and partly from scholarships supplied by public grants. Wherever it is possible, wherever, that is, their scale of charges is not too high, or their situation not too unsuitable, existing schools of good repute should be adopted as the *Royal Schools*. Schools such as Mr. Woodard's, such as King Edward's School at Birmingham, such as the Collegiate School at Liverpool, at once occur to one as suitable for this adoption; it would confer upon them, besides its other advantages, a public character which they are now without. Probably the very best medicine which could be devised for the defects of Eton, Harrow, and the other schools which the Royal Commissioners have been scrutinising, would be the juxtaposition, and, to a certain extent, the competition, of establishments of this kind. No wise man will desire to see root-and-branch work made with schools like Eton or Harrow, or to see them diverted from the function which they at present discharge, and, on the whole, usefully. Great subversive changes would here be out of place; it is an addition of new that our secondary instruction wants, not a demolition of old, or, at least, not of this old. But to this old I cannot doubt that the apparition and operation of this desirable new would give a very fruitful stimulus; as this new, on its part, would certainly be very much influenced and benefited by the old.

The repartition of the charge of this new secondary instruction, the mode of its assessment, the constitution of the bodies for regulating the new system, the proportion and character of functions to be assigned to local and to central authority respectively, these are matters of detail and arrangement which it is foreign to my business here to discuss, and, I hope, quite foreign to my disposition to haggle and wrangle about. They are to be settled upon a due consideration of circumstances, after an attentive scrutiny of our existing means of operation, and a discriminating review of the practice of other countries. In general, if it is agreed to give a public and coherent organisation to secondary instruction, few will dispute that its particular direction, in different localities, is best committed to local bodies, properly constituted, with a power of supervision by an impartial central authority, and of resort to this authority in the last instance. Of local bodies, bad or good, administering education, we have already plenty of specimens in this country; it would be difficult for the wit of man to devise a better governing body for its purpose than the trustees of Rugby School, or a worse governing body than the trustees of Bedford School. To reject the bad in the examples offering themselves, to use the good, and to use it with just regard to the present purpose, is the thing needful. Undoubtedly these are important matters; but undoubtedly, also, it is not difficult to settle them properly; not difficult, I mean, for ordinary good sense, and ordinary good temper. The intelligence, fairness, and moderation which, in practical matters, our countrymen know so well how to exercise, make one feel quite easy in leaving these common-sense arrangements to them.

I am more anxious about the danger of having the whole question misconceived, of having false issues raised upon it. One of these false issues I have already noticed. People say: "After "all, your Toulouse Lyceum is not so good as "Eton." (But the Toulouse Lyceum is for the middle class, Eton for the upper class. I will allow that the upper class, amongst us, is very well taken care of, in the way of schools, already. But is the middle class?) The Lyceum loses, perhaps, if compared with Eton; but does it not gain if compared with the "Classical and Com-

"mercial Academy?" And it is with this that the comparison is instituted. Again, the French Lyceum is reproached with its barrack life, its want of country air and exercise, its dismalness, its rigidity, its excessive supervision. But these defects do not come to secondary instruction from its connexion with the State; they are not necessary results of that connexion; they come to French secondary instruction from the common French and continental habitudes in the training of children and school-boys—habitudes that do not enough regard physical well-being and play. They may be remedied in France, and men's attention is now strongly drawn to them there; there has even been a talk of moving the Lyceums into the country, though this would have its inconveniences. But, at any rate, these defects need not attend the public establishment of secondary instruction in England, and assuredly, with our notions of training, they would not attend them. Again, it is said that France is a despotically-governed country, and that its Lyceums are a part of its despotism. But Switzerland is not a despotically-governed country, and it has its Lyceums just as much as France. Again, it is said that in France the Lyceums are the only schools allowed to exist, that this is monopoly and tyranny, and that the Lyceums themselves suffer by the want of competition. There is some exaggeration in this complaint, as the existence of Sorèze, and other places like Sorèze, testifies; still the restraints put upon private enterprise in founding schools in France, are, no doubt, mischievously strict; the refusal of the requisite authorisation for opening a private school is often vexatious; the Lyceums would really be benefited by the proximity of other, and sometimes rival, schools. But who supposes that any check would ever be put, in England, upon private enterprise in founding schools? Who supposes that the authorisation demanded in France for opening a private school would ever be demanded in England, that it would ever be possible to demand it, that it would ever be desirable? Who supposes that all the benefits of a public establishment of instruction are not to be obtained without it? It is for what it does itself that this establishment is so desirable, not for what it prevents others from doing. Its letting others alone does not prevent it from itself having a most useful work to do, and a work which can be done by no one else. The most zealous friends of free instruction upon the Continent feel this. One of the ablest of them, M. Dollfus, lately published in the *Revue Germanique* some most interesting remarks on the defects of the French school system, as at present regulated. He demands freedom for private persons to open schools without any authorisation at all. But does he contest the right of the State to have its own schools, to make a public establishment of instruction? So far from it, he treats this as a right beyond all contestation, as a clear duty. He treats as certain, too, the right of the State to inspect all private schools once opened, though he denies the right, and the good policy, of its putting the present obstacles in the way of opening them.

But there is a catchword which, I know, will be used against me. England is the country of cries and catchwords; a country where public life is so much carried on by means of parties must be. That English public life should be carried on as it is, I believe to be an excellent thing, but it is certain that all modes of life have their special inconveniences, and every sensible man, however much he may hold a particular way of life to be the best, and may be bent on adhering to it, will yet always be sedulous to guard himself against its inconveniences. One of these is, certainly, in English public life, the prevalence of cries and catchwords, which are very apt to receive an application, or to be used with an absoluteness, which do not belong to them; and then they tend to narrow our spirit and to hurt our practice. It is good to make a catchword of this sort come down from its stronghold of commonplace, to force it to move about before us in the open country, and to show us its real strength. Such a catchword as this: *The State had better leave things alone.* One constantly hears that as an absolute maxim; now, as an absolute maxim, it has really no force at all. The absolute maxims are those which carry to man's spirit their own demonstration with them; such propositions as, *Duty is the law of human life, Man is morally free,* and so on. The proposition, *The State had better leave things alone,* carries no such demonstration with it; it has, therefore, no absolute force; it merely conveys a notion which certain people have generalised from certain facts which have come under their observation, and which, by a natural vice of the human mind, they are then prone to apply absolutely. Some things the State had better leave alone, others it had better not. Is this particular thing one of these, or one of those?—that, as to any particular thing, is the right question. Now, I say, that education is one of those things which the State ought not to leave alone, which it ought to establish. It is said that in education given, wholly or in part, by the State, there is something eleemosynary, pauperising, degrading; that the self-respect and manly energy of those receiving it are likely to become impaired, as I have said that the manly energy of those who are too much made to feel their dependence upon a parental benefactor, is apt to become impaired. Well, now, is this so? Is a citizen's relation to the State that of a dependent to a parental benefactor? By no means; it is that of a member in a partnership to the whole firm. The citizens of a State, the members of a society, are really a partnership; "a " partnership," as Burke nobly says, " in all " science, in all art, in every virtue, in all perfec- " tion." Towards this great final design of their connexion, they apply the aids which co-operative association can give them. This applied to education will, undoubtedly, give the middling person a better schooling than his own individual unaided resources could give him; but he is not thereby humiliated, he is not degraded; he is wisely and usefully turning his associated condition to the best account. Considering his end and destination, he is bound so to turn it; certainly he has a right so to turn it. Certainly he has a right—to quote Burke again—"to a fair "portion of all which society, *with all its combi-* "*nations of skill and force*, can do in his favour." Men in civil society have the right—to quote Burke yet once more (one cannot quote him too often)—as "to the acquisitions of their parents "and to the fruits of their own industry," so also "*to the improvement of their offspring, to instruc-* "*tion in life*, and to consolation in death."

How vain, then, and how meaningless, to tell a man who, for the instruction of his offspring, receives aid from the State, that he is humiliated! Humiliated by receiving help for himself as an individual from himself in his corporate and associated capacity! help to which his own money, as a tax-payer, contributes, and for which, as a result of the joint energy and intelligence of the whole community in employing its powers, he himself deserves some of the praise! He is no more humiliated than one is humiliated by being on the foundation of the Charterhouse or of Winchester, or by holding a scholarship or fellowship at Oxford or Cambridge. Nay (if there be any humiliation here), not so much. For the amount of benefaction, the amount of obligation, the amount, therefore, I suppose, of humiliation, diminishes as the public character of the aid becomes more undeniable. He is no more humiliated than when he crosses London Bridge, or walks down the King's Road, or visits the British Museum. But it is one of the extraordinary inconsistencies of some English people in this matter, that they keep all their cry of humiliation and degradation for help which the State offers. A man is not pauperised, is not degraded, is not oppressively obliged, by taking aid for his son's schooling from Mr. Woodard's subscribers, or from the next squire, or from the next rector, or from the next ironmonger, or from the next druggist; he is only pauperised when he takes it from the State, when he helps to give it himself!

This matter of State-intervention in the establishment of public instruction is so beset with misrepresentation and misconception, that I must, before concluding, go into it a little more fully. I want the middle classes (it is for them, above all, I write), the middle classes so deeply concerned in this matter, so numerous, so right-intentioned, so powerful, to look at the thing with impartial regard to its simple reason and to its present policy.

THE State mars everything which it touches, say some. It attempts to do things for private people, and private people could do them a great deal better for themselves. "The State," says the *Times*, "can hardly aid education without "cramping and warping its growth, and mis-"chievously interfering with the laws of its "natural development." "Why should persons "in Downing Street," asks Dr. Temple, "be at "all better qualified than the rest of the world "for regulating these matters?" Happily, however, this agency, at once so mischievous and so blundering, is in our country little used. "In "this country," says the *Times* again, "people "cannot complain of the State, because the "State never promised them anything, *but, on* "*the contrary, always told them it could do them* "*no good*. The result is, none are fed with false "hopes." So it is, and so it will be to the end. "This is something more than a system with us; "*it is usage, it is a necessity*. We shall go on "for ages doing as we have done."

Whether this really is so or not, it seems as if

it *ought* not to be so. "Government," says Burke (to go back to Burke again), "is a contri-" vance of human wisdom to provide for human " wants. Men have a right that these wants " should be provided for by this wisdom." We are a free people, we have made our own Government. Our own wisdom has planned our contrivance for providing for our own wants. And what sort of a contrivance has our wisdom made? According to the *Times*, a contrivance of which the highest merit is, that it candidly avows its own impotency. It does not provide for our wants, but then it "always told us" it could not provide for them. It does not fulfil its function, but then it "never fed us with false hopes" that it would. It is perfectly useless, but perfectly candid. And it will always remain what it is now; it will always be a contrivance which contrives nothing: this with us "is usage, it is a " necessity." Good heavens! what a subject for self-congratulation! What bitterer satire on us and our institutions could our worst enemy invent?

Dr. Temple may well ask, "Why should per-" sons in Downing Street be at all better qualified " than the rest of the world for regulating such " matters as education?" Why should not a sporting rector in Norfolk, or a fanatical cobbler in Northamptonshire, be just as good a judge of what is wise, equitable, and expedient in public education, as an Education Minister? Why, indeed? The Education Minister is a part of our contrivance for providing for our wants, and we have seen what that contrivance is worth. It might have been expected, perhaps, that in contriving a provision for a special want, we should have sought for some one with a special skill. But we know that our contrivance will do no good, so we may as well let Nimrod manage as Numa.

From whence can have arisen, in this country, such contemptuous disparagement of the efficiency and utility of State-action? Whence such studied depreciation of an agency which to Burke, or, indeed, to any reflecting man, appears an agency of the greatest possible power and value? For several reasons. In the first place, the government of this country is, and long has been, in the hands of the aristocratic class. Where the aristocracy is a small oligarchy, able to find employment for all its members in the administration of the State, it is not the enemy, but the friend of State-action; for State-action is then but its own action under another name, and it is itself directly aggrandised by all that aggrandises the State. But where, as in this country, the aristocracy is a very large class, by no means conterminous with the executive, but overlapping it and spreading far beyond it, it is the natural enemy rather than the friend of State-action; for only a small part of its members can directly administer the State, and it is not for the interest of the remainder to give to this small part an excessive preponderance. (Nay, this small part will not be apt to seek it; for its interest in its order is permanent, while its interest in State-function is transitory, and it obeys an instinct which attaches it by preference to its order.) The more an aristocracy has of that profound political sense by which the English aristocracy is so much distinguished, the more its members obey this instinct; and, by doing so, they signally display their best virtues, moderation, prudence, sagacity; they prevent fruitful occasions of envy, dissension, and strife; they do much to insure the permanence of their order, its harmonious action, and continued predominance. A tradition unfavourable to much State-action in home concerns (foreign are another thing) is thus insensibly established in the Government itself. This tradition, this essentially aristocratic sentiment, gains even those members of the Government who are not of the aristocratic class. In the beginning they are overpowered by it; in the end they share it. When the shepherd Daphnis first arrives in heaven, he naturally bows to the august traditions of his new sphere—*candidus insuetum miratur limen Olympi.* By the time the novelty of his situation has worn off, he has come to think just as the immortals do; he is now by conviction the foe of State-interference; the worthy Daphnis is all for letting things alone—*amat bonus otia Daphnis.*

Far from trying to encroach upon individual liberty, far from seeking to get everything into its own hands, such a Government has a natural and instinctive tendency to limit its own functions. It turns away from offers of increased responsibility or activity; it deprecates them. To propose increased responsibility and activity to an aristocratic Government is the worst possible way of paying one's court to it. The *Times* is its genuine mouthpiece, when it says that the business of Government, in domestic concerns, is negative—to prevent disorder, jobbery, and extravagance; that it need "have no "notion of securing the future, not even of "regulating the present;" that it may and ought to "leave the course of events to regulate "itself, and trust the future to the security of "the unknown laws of human nature and the "unseen influences of higher powers." This is the true aristocratic theory of civil government; to have recourse as little as possible to State-action, to the collective action of the community; to leave as much as possible to the individual, to local government. And why? Because the members of an aristocratic class are preponderating individuals, with the local government in their hands. No wonder that they do not wish to see the State overshadowing them and ordering them about. Since the feudal epoch, the palmy time of local government, the State has overlaid individual action quite enough. Mr. Adderley remembers with a sigh that "Houses "of Correction were once voluntary institutions." Go a little further back, and the court of justice was a voluntary institution; the gallows was a voluntary institution; voluntary, I mean, in Mr. Adderley's sense of the word voluntary—not depending on the State, but on the local government, on the lord of the soil, on the preponderating individual. The State has overlaid the feudal gallows, it has overlaid the feudal court of justice, it has overlaid the feudal House of Correction, and finally, says Mr. Adderley, "it has overlaid "our school-system." What will it do next?

In the aristocratic class, whose members mainly compose and whose sentiment powerfully pervades the executive of this country, jealousy of State-action is, I repeat, an intelligible, a profoundly natural feeling. That, amid the temptations of office, they have remained true to it is a proof of their practical sense, their sure tact, their moderation—the qualities which go to make that *governing spirit* for which the English aristocracy is so remarkable. And perhaps this governing spirit of theirs is destined still to stand them in good stead through all the new and changing development of modern society. Perhaps it will give them the tact to discern the critical moment at which it becomes of urgent national importance that an agency, not in itself very agreeable to them, should be used more freely than heretofore. They have had the virtue to prefer the general interest of their order to personal temptations of aggrandising themselves through this agency; perhaps they will be capable of the still higher virtue of admitting, in the general interest of their country, this agency, in spite of the natural prejudices and the seeming immediate interest of their own order. Already there are indications that this is not impossible. No thoughtful observer can have read Lord Derby's remarks last session on the regulation of our railway system, can have followed the course of a man like Sir John Pakington on the Education question, can have watched the disposition of the country gentlemen on a measure like Mr. Gladstone's Government Annuities Bill, without recognising that political instinct, that governing spirit, which often, in the aristocratic class of this country, is wiser both than the unelastic pedantry of theorising Liberalism, and than their own prejudices.

The working classes have no antipathy to State-action. Against this, or against anything else, indeed, presented to them in close connexion with some proceeding which they dislike, it is, no doubt, quite possible to get them to raise a cry; but to the thing itself they have no objection. Quite the contrary. They often greatly embarrass their Liberal friends and patrons from other classes, one of whose favourite catchwords is *no State-interference*, by their resolute refusal to adopt this Shibboleth, to embrace this article of their patrons' creed. They will join with them in their Liberalism, not in their crotchets. Left to themselves, they are led, as by their plain interest, so, too, by their natural disposition, to welcome the action of the State in their behalf.

It is the middle class that has been this action's great enemy. (And originally it had good reason to be its enemy. In the youth and early manhood of the English middle class, the action of the State was at the service of an ecclesiastical party.) This party used the power of the State to secure their own predominance, and to enforce conformity to their own tenets. The stronghold of Nonconformity then, as now, was in the middle class; in its struggle to repel the conformity forced upon it, the middle class underwent great suffering and injustice; and it has never forgotten them. It has never forgotten that the hand which smote it—the hand which did the bidding of its High Church and prelatical enemies—was the hand of the State. It has confronted the State with hostile jealousy ever since. The State tried to do it violence, so it does not love the State; the State failed to subdue it, so it does not respect the State. It regards it with something of aversion and something of contempt. It professes the desire to limit its functions as much as possible, to restrict its action to matters where it is indispensably necessary, to make of it a mere tax-collector and policeman—the hewer of wood and drawer of water to the community.

There is another cause also which indisposes the English middle class to increased action on the part of the State. M. Amédée Thierry, in his "History of the Gauls," observes, in contrasting the Gaulish and Germanic races, that the first is characterised by the instinct of intelligence and mobility, and by the preponderant action of individuals; the second, by the instinct of discipline and order, and by the preponderant action of bodies of men. This general law of M. Thierry's has to submit to many limitations, but there is a solid basis of truth in it. Applying the law to a people mainly of German blood like ourselves, we shall best perceive its truth by regarding the middle class of the nation. Multitudes, all the world over, have a good deal in common; aristocracies, all the world over, have a good deal in common. The peculiar national form and habit exist in the masses at the bottom of society in a loose, rudimentary, potential state; in the few at the top of society, in a state modified and reduced by various culture. The man of the multitude has not yet solidified into the typical Englishman; the man of the aristocracy has been etherealised out of him. The typical Englishman is to be looked for in the middle class. And there we shall find him, with a complexion not ill-suiting M. Thierry's law; with a spirit not very open to new ideas, and not easily ravished by them; not, therefore, a great enthusiast for universal progress, but with a strong love of discipline and order,—that is, of keeping things settled, and much as they are; and with a disposition, instead of lending himself to the onward-looking statesman and legislator, to act with bodies of men of his own kind, whose aims and efforts reach no further than his own. Poverty and hope make man the friend of ideals, therefore the multitude has a turn for ideals; culture and genius make man the friend of ideals, therefore the gifted or highly-trained few have a turn for ideals. The middle class has the whet neither of poverty nor of culture; it is not ill-off in the things of the body, and it is not highly trained in the things of the mind; therefore it has little turn for ideals: it is self-satisfied. This is a chord in the nature of the English middle class which seldom fails, when struck, to give an answer, and which some people are never weary of striking. All the variations which are played on the endless theme of *local self-government* rely on this chord. Hardly any local government is, in truth, in this country, exercised by the middle class; almost the whole of it is exercised by the aristocratic class. Every locality in France—that country which our middle class is taught so much to compassionate—has a genuine municipal government, in which the middle class has its due share; and by this municipal government all matters of local concern (schools among the number) are regulated; not a country parish in England has any effective government of this kind at all. But what is meant by the habit of local self-government, on which our middle class is so incessantly felicitated, is its habit of voluntary combination, in bodies of its own arranging, for purposes of its own choosing—purposes to be carried out within the limits fixed for a private association by its own powers. When the middle class is solemnly warned against State-interference, lest it should destroy "the habit of " self-reliance and love of local self-government," it is this habit, and the love of it, that are meant. When we are told that "nothing can be more " dangerous than these constant attempts on the "part of the Government to take from the people "the management of its own concerns," this is the sort of management of our own concerns that is meant; not the management of them by a regular local government, but the management of them by chance private associations. It is our habit of acting through these associations which, says Mr. Roebuck, saves us from being "a set of "helpless imbeciles, totally incapable of attending "to our own interests." It is in the event of this habit being at all altered that, according to the same authority, "the greatness of this country is "gone."* And the middle class, to whom that habit is familiar and very dear, will never be insensible to language of this sort.

Finally, the English middle class has a strong practical sense and habit of affairs, and it sees that things managed by the Government are often managed ill. It sees them treated some-

---

* Mr. Roebuck, in his recent excellent speech at Sheffield, has shown that in popular education, at any rate, he does not mean these maxims to apply without restriction. But perhaps it is a little incautious for a public man ever to throw out, without guarding himself, maxims of this kind; for, on the one hand, in this country such maxims are sure never to be lost sight of; on the other, but too many people are sure always to be prone to use them amiss, and to push their application much fnrther than it ought to go.

times remissly, sometimes vexatiously ; now with a paralysing want of fruitful energy, now with an over-busy fussiness, with rigidity, with formality, without due consideration of special circumstances. Here, too, it finds a motive disinclining it to trust State-action, and leading it to give a willing ear to those who declaim against it.

Now, every one of these motives of distrust is respectable. Every one of them has, or once had, a solid ground. Every one of them points to some virtue in those actuated by it, which is not to be suppressed, but to find true conditions for its exercise. The English middle class was quite right in repelling State-action, when the State suffered itself to be made an engine of the High Church party to persecute Nonconformists. It gave an excellent lesson to the State in so doing. It rendered a valuable service to liberty of thought and to all human freedom. If State-action now threatened to lend itself to one religious party against another, the middle class would be quite right in again thwarting and confining it. But can it be said that the State now shows the slightest disposition to take such a course ? Is such a course the course towards which the modern spirit carries the State ? Does not the State show, more and more, the resolution to hold the balance perfectly fair between religious parties? The middle class has it in its own power, more than any other class, to confirm the State in this resolution. This class has the power to make it thoroughly sure—in organising, for instance, any new system of public instruction—that the State shall treat all religious persuasions with exactly equal fairness. If, instead of holding aloof, it will now but give its aid to make State-action equitable, it can make it so.

Again, as to the "habits of self-reliance and "the love of local self-government." People talk of Government *interference*, Government *control*, as if State-action were necessarily something imposed upon them from without; something despotic and self-originated; something which took no account of their will, and left no freedom to their activity. Can any one really suppose that, in a country like this, State-action—in education, for instance—can ever be that, unless we choose to make it so? We can give it what form we will. We can make it our agent, not our master. In modern societies the agency of the State, in certain matters, is so indispensable, that it will manage, with or without our common consent, to come into operation somehow; but when it has introduced itself without the common consent—when a great body, like the middle class, will have nothing to say to it—then its course is indeed likely enough to be not straightforward, its operation not satisfactory. But, by all of us consenting to it, we remove any danger of this kind. By really agreeing to deal in our collective and corporate character with education, we can form ourselves into the best and most efficient of voluntary societies for managing it. We can make State-action upon it a genuine local government of it, the faithful but potent expression of our own activity. We can make the central Government that mere court of disinterested review and correction, which every sensible man would always be glad to have for his own activity. We shall have all our self-reliance and individual action still (in this country we shall always have plenty of them, and the parts will always be more likely to tyrannise over the whole than the whole over the parts), but we shall have had the good sense to turn them to account by a powerful, but still voluntary, organisation. Our beneficence will be "beneficence "acting *by rule*" (that is Burke's definition of law, as instituted by a free society), and all the more effective for that reason. Must this make us "a set of helpless imbeciles, totally incapable "of attending to our own interests?" Is this "a grievous blow aimed at the independence "of the English character?" Is "English self-"reliance and independence" to be perfectly satisfied with what it produces already without this organisation? In middle class education it produces, without it, the educational home and the classical and commercial academy. Are we to be proud of that? Are we to be satisfied with that? Is "the greatness of this country" to be seen in that? But it will be said that, awakening to a sense of the badness of our middle class education, we are beginning to improve it. Undoubtedly we are; and the most certain sign of that awakening, of those beginnings of improvement, is the disposition to resort to a public agency, to "beneficence working *by rule*," to help us on faster with it. When we really begin to care about a matter of this kind, we cannot help turning to the most efficient agency at our disposal. Clap-trap and commonplace lose their power over us; we begin to see that, if State action has often its inconveniences, our self-reliance and independence are best shown in so arranging our State-action as to guard against those inconveniences, not in foregoing State-action for fear of them. So it was in elementary education. Mr. Baines says that this was already beginning to improve, when Government interfered with it. Why, it was because we were all beginning to take a real interest in it, beginning to improve it, that we turned to Government—to ourselves in our corporate character—to get it improved faster. So long as we did not care much about it, we let it go its own way, and kept singing Mr. Roebuck's fine old English stave about "self-reliance." We kept crying just as he cries now: "nobody has the same interest "to do well for a man as he himself has." That was all very pleasant so long as we cared not a rush whether the people were educated or no. The moment we began to concern ourselves about this, we asked ourselves what our song was worth. We asked ourselves how the bringing up of our labourers and artisans—they "doing "for themselves," and "nobody having the same "interest to do well for a man as he himself has" —was being done. We found it was being done detestably. Then we asked ourselves whether casual, precarious, voluntary beneficence, or "beneficence acting by rule," was the better agency for doing it better. We asked ourselves if we could not employ our public resources on this concern, if we could not make our beneficence act upon it by rule, without losing our "habits of "self-reliance," without "aiming a grievous blow "at the independence of the English character." We found that we could; we began to do it; and we left Mr. Baines to sing in the wilderness.

Finally, as to the objection that our State-action—our "beneficence working by rule"—often bungles and does its work badly. No wonder it does. The imperious necessities of modern society force it, more or less, even in this country, into play; but it is exercised by a class to whose cherished instincts it is opposed—the aristocratic class; and it is watched by a class to whose cherished prejudices it is opposed—the middle class. It is hesitatingly exercised and jealously watched. It therefore works without courage, cordiality, or belief in itself. Under its present conditions it must work so, and, working so, it must often bungle. But it need not work so; and the moment the middle class abandons its attitude of jealous aversion, the moment they frankly put their hand to it, the moment they adopt it as an instrument to do them service, it will work so no longer. Then it will not bungle; then, if it is applied, say, to education, it will not be fussy, baffling, and barren; it will bring to bear on this concern the energy and strong practical sense of the middle class itself.

But the middle class must make it do this. They must not expect others to do the business for them. It is they whose interest is concerned in its being done, and they must do it for themselves. Why should the upper class—the aristocratic class—do it for them? What motive—except the distant and not very peremptory one of their general political sense, their instinct for taking the course which, for the whole country's sake, ought to be taken—have the aristocratic class to impel them to go counter to all their natural maxims, nay, and to all their seeming interest? They do not want new schools for their children. The great public schools of the country are theirs already. Their numbers are not such as to overflow these few really public schools; their fortunes are such as to make the expensiveness of these schools a matter of indifference to them. The Royal Commissioners, whose report has just appeared, do not, indeed, give a very brilliant picture of the book-learning of these schools. But it is not the book-learning (easy to be improved if there is a will to improve it) that this class make their first care; they make their first care the tone, temper, and habits generated in these schools. So long as they generate a public spirit, a free spirit, a high spirit, a governing spirit, they are not ill-satisfied. Their children are fitted to succeed them in the government of the country. Why should they concern themselves to change this state of things? Why should they create competitors for their own children? Why should they labour to endow another class with those great instruments of power—a public spirit, a free spirit, a high spirit, a governing spirit? Why should they do violence to that distaste for State-action, which, in an aristocratic class, is natural and instinctive, for the benefit of the middle class?

No; the middle class must do this work for themselves. From them must come the demand for the satisfaction of a want that is theirs. They must leave off being frightened at shadows. They may keep (I hope they always will keep) the maxim that self-reliance and independence are the most invaluable of blessings, that the great end of society is the perfecting of the individual, the fullest, freest, and worthiest development of the individual's activity. But that the individual may be perfected, that his activity may be worthy, he must often learn to quit old habits to adopt new, to go out of himself, to transform himself. It was said, and truly said, of one of the most unwearied and successful strivers after human perfection that have ever lived—Wilhelm von Humboldt—that it was a joy to him to feel himself modified by the operation of a foreign influence. And this may well be a joy to a man whose centre of character and whose moral force are once securely established. Through this he makes growth in perfection. Through this he enlarges his being and fills up gaps in it; he unlearns old prejudices and learns new excellences; he makes advance towards inward light and freedom. Societies may use this means of perfection as well as individuals, and it is a characteristic (perhaps the best characteristic) of our age, that they are using it more and more. Let us look at our neighbour, France. What strikes a thoughtful observer most in modern France, is the great, wide breach which is being made in the old French mind; the strong flow with which a foreign thought is pouring in and mixing with it. There is an extraordinary increase in the number of German and English books read there, books the most unlike possible to the native literary growth of France. There is a growing disposition there to pull to pieces old stock French commonplaces, and to put a bridle upon old stock French habitudes. France will not, and should not, like some English liberals, run a-muck against State-action altogether; but she shows a tendency to control her excessive State-action, to reduce it within just limits where it has overpassed them, to make a larger part for free local activity and for individuals. She will not, and should not, like Sir Archibald Alison, cry down her great Revolution as the work of Satan; but she shows more and more the power to discern the real faults of that Revolution, the real part of delusion, impotence, and transitoriness in the work of '89 or of '91, and to profit by that discernment.

Our middle class has secured for itself that centre of character and that moral force which are, I have said, the indispensable basis upon which perfection is to be founded. To securing them, its vigour in resisting the State, when the State tried to tyrannise over it, has contributed not a little. In this sense, it may be said to have made way towards perfection by repelling the State's hand. Now it has to enlarge and to adorn its spirit. I cannot seriously argue with those who deny that the independence and free action of the middle class is now, in this country, immutably secure; I cannot treat the notion of the State now overriding it and doing violence to it, as anything but a vain chimera. Well, then, if the State can (as it can) be of service to the middle class in the work of enlarging its mind and adorning its spirit, it will now make way towards perfection by taking the State's hand. State-action is not in itself unfavourable to the individual's perfection, to his attaining his fullest development. So far from it, it is in ancient Greece, where State-action was omnipresent, that we see the individual at his very highest pitch of free and fair activity. This is because, in Greece, the individual was strong enough to fashion the State into an instrument of his own perfection, to make it serve, with a thousand times his own power, towards his own ends. He was not enslaved by it, he did not annihilate it, but he used it. Where, in modern nations, the State has maimed and crushed individual activity, it has been by operating as an alien, exterior power in the community, a power not originated by the community to serve the common weal, but entrenched among them as a conqueror with a weal of its own to serve. Just because the vigour and sturdiness of the people of this country have prevented, and will always prevent, the State from being anything of this kind, I believe we, more than any modern people, have the power of renewing, in our national life, the example of Greece. I believe that we, and our American kinsmen, are specially fit to apply State-action with advantage, because we are specially sure to apply it voluntarily.

Two things must, I think, strike any one who attentively regards the English middle class at this moment. One is the intellectual ferment which is taking place, or rather, which is beginning to take place, amongst them. It is only in its commencement as yet; but it shows itself at a number of points, and bids fair to become a great power. The importance of a change, placing in the great middle class the centre of the intellectual life of this country, can hardly be over-estimated. I have been reproved for saying that the culture and intellectual life of our highest class seem to me to have somewhat flagged since the last century. That is my opinion, indeed, and all that I see and hear strengthens rather than shakes it. The culture of this class is not what it used to be. Their value for high culture, their belief in its importance, is not what it used to be. One may see it in the public schools, one may see it in the universities. Whence come the deadness, the want of intellectual life, the poverty of acquirement after years of schooling, which the Commissioners, in their remarkable and interesting report, show us so prevalent in our most distinguished public schools? What gives to play and amusement, both there and at the universities, their present overweening importance, so that home critics cry out: "The real studies of "Oxford are its games," and foreign critics cry out: "At Oxford the student is still the mere "school-boy"? The most experienced and acute of Oxford heads of houses told me himself, that when he spoke to an undergraduate the other day about trying for some distinguished scholarship, the answer he got was: "Oh, the men "from the great schools don't care for those "things now; the men who care about them are "the men from Marlborough, Cheltenham, and "the second-rate schools." Whence, I say, does this slackness, this sleep of the mind, come, except from a torpor of intellectual life, a dearth of ideas, an indifference to fine culture or disbelief in its necessity, spreading through the bulk of our highest class, and influencing its rising generation? People talk as if the culture of this class had only changed; the Greek and Roman classics, they say, are no longer in vogue as they were in Lord Chesterfield's time. Well, if this class had only gone from one source of high culture to another; if only, instead of reading Homer and Cicero, it now read Goethe and Montesquieu;—but it does not; it reads the *Times* and the *Agricultural Journal.* And it devotes itself to practical life. And it amuses itself. It is not its rising generation only which loves play; never in all its history has our whole highest class shown such zeal for enjoying life, for amusing itself. It would be absurd to make this a matter of reproach against it. The triumphs of material progress multiply the means of material enjoyment; they attract all classes, more and more, to taste of this enjoyment; on the highest class, which possesses in the amplest measure these means, they must needs exercise this attraction very powerfully. But every thoughtful observer can perceive that the ardour for amusement and enjoyment, often educative and quickening to a toil-numbed working class or a strait-laced middle class, whose great want is expansion, tends to become enervative and weakening to an aristocratic class—a class which must rule by superiority of all kinds, superiority not to be won without contention of spirit and a certain severity. I think, therefore, both that the culture of our highest class has declined, and that this declension, though natural and venial, impairs its power.

Yet in this vigorous country everything has a wonderful ability for self-restoration, and he would be a bold prophet who should deny that the culture of our highest class may recover itself. But however this may be, there is no doubt that a liberal culture, a fulness of intellectual life, in the middle class, is a far more important matter, a far more efficacious stimulant to national progress, than the same powers in an aristocratic class. Whatever may be its culture, an aristocratic class will always have at bottom, like the young man in Scripture with great possessions, an inaptitude for ideas; but, besides this, high culture or ardent intelligence, pervading a large body of the community, acquire a breadth of basis, a sum of force, an energy of central heat for radiating further, which they can never possess when they pervade a small upper class only. It is when such a broad basis is obtained, that individual genius gets its proper nutriment, and is animated to put forth its best powers; this is the secret of rich and beautiful epochs in national life; the epoch of Pericles in Greece, the epoch of Michael Angelo in Italy, the epoch of Shakspeare in England. Our actual middle class has not yet, certainly, the fine culture, or the living intelligence, which quickened great bodies of men at these epochs; but it has the forerunner, the preparer, the indispensable initiator; it is traversed by a strong intellectual ferment. It is the middle class which has real mental ardour, real curiosity; it is the middle class which is the great reader; that immense literature of the day which we see surging up all round us,—literature the absolute value of which it is almost impossible to rate too humbly, literature hardly a word of which will reach, or deserves to reach, the future,—it is the middle class which calls it forth, and its evocation is at least a sign of a widespread mental movement in that class. Will this movement go on and become fruitful: will it conduct the middle class to a high and commanding pitch of culture and intelligence? That depends on the sensibility which the middle class has for *perfection;* that depends on its power to *transform itself.*

And it is not yet manifest how far it possesses this power. For—and here I pass to the second of those two things which particularly, I have said, strike any one who observes the English middle class just now—in its public action this class has hitherto shown only the power and disposition to *affirm itself*, not at all the power and disposition to *transform itself*. That, indeed, is one of the deep-seated instincts of human nature, but of vulgar human nature—of human nature not high-souled and aspiring after perfection—to esteem itself for what it is, to try to establish itself just as it is, to try even to impose itself with its stock of habitudes, pettinesses, narrownesses, shortcomings of every kind, on the rest of the world as a conquering power. But nothing has really a right to be satisfied with itself, to be and remain itself, except that which has reached perfection; and nothing has the right to impose itself on the rest of the world as a conquering force, except that which is of higher perfection than the rest of the world. And such is the fundamental constitution of human affairs, that the measure of right proves also, in the end, the measure of power. Before the English middle class can have the right or the power to assert itself absolutely, it must have greatly perfected itself. It has been jokingly said of this class, that all which the best of it cared for was summed up in this alliterative phrase—*Business and Bethels:* and that all which the rest of it cared for was the *Business* without the *Bethels*. No such jocose and slighting words can convey any true sense of what the religion of the English middle class has really been to it ; what a source of vitality, energy, and persistent vigour. "They who wait on the Lord," says Isaiah, in words not less true than they are noble, "*shall renew their strength ;*" and the English middle class owes to its religion not only comfort in the past, but also a vast latent force of unworn life and strength for future progress. But the Puritanism of the English middle class, which has been so great an element of strength to them, has by no means brought them to perfection ; nay, by the rigid mould in which it has cast their spirit, it has kept them back from perfection. The most that can be said of it is, that it has supplied a stable basis on which to build perfection ; it has given them character, though it has not given them culture, But it is in making endless additions to itself, in the endless expansion of its powers, in endless growth in wisdom and beauty, that the spirit of the human race finds its ideal ; to reach this ideal, culture is an indispensable aid, and that is the true value of culture. The life of aristocracies, with its large and free use of the world, its conversance with great affairs, its exemption from sordid cares, its liberation from the humdrum provincial round, its external splendour and refinement, is a kind of outward shadow of this ideal, a prophecy of it; and there lies the secret of the charm of aristocracies, and of their power over men's minds. In a country like England, the middle class, with its industry and its Puritanism, and nothing more, will never be able to make way beyond a certain point, will never be able to divide power with the aristocratic class, much less to win for itself a preponderance of power. While it only tries to affirm its actual self, to impose its actual self, it has no charm for men's minds, and can achieve no great triumphs. And this is all it attempts at present. The Conservative reaction, of which we hear so much just now, is in great part merely a general indisposition to let the middle-class spirit, working by its old methods, and having only its old self to give us,.establish itself at all points and become master of the situation. Particularly on Church questions is this true. In this sphere of religion, where feeling and beauty are so all-important, we shrink from giving to the middle-class spirit, limited as we see it, with its sectarianism, its under-culture, its intolerance, its bitterness, its unloveliness, too much its own way. Before we give it quite its own way, we insist on its making itself into something larger, newer, more fruitful. This is what the recent Church-Rate divisions really mean, and the lovers of perfection, therefore, may accept them without displeasure. They are the voice of the nation crying to the *untransformed* middle class (if it will receive it) with a voice of thunder: "The future is not yours!"

And let me say, in passing, that the indifference, so irritating to some persons, with which European opinion has received the break-up of the old American Union has at bottom a like ground. I put the question of slavery on one side; so far as the resolution of that question depends on the issue of the conflict between the North and the South, every one may wish this party or that to prevail. But Mr. Bright and Mr. Cobden extol the old American Republic as something interesting and admirable in itself, and are displeased with those who are not afflicted at its disaster, and not jealous for its restoration. Mr. Bright is an orator of genius; Mr. Cobden is a man of splendid understanding. But why do they refuse to perceive, that, apart from all class-jealousy of aristocracies towards a democratic republic, there existed in the most impartial and thoughtful minds a profound dissatisfaction with the spirit and tendencies of the old American Union, a strong aversion to their unchecked triumph, a sincere wish for the disciplining and correcting of them? And what were the old United States but a colossal expression of the English middle-class spirit, somewhat more accessible to ideas there than here, because of the democratic air it breathed, much more arrogant and overweening there than here, because of the absence of all check and counterpoise to it—but there, as here, full of rawness, hardness, and imperfection; there, as here, greatly needing to be liberalised, enlarged, and ennobled, before it could with advantage be suffered to assert itself absolutely? All the energy and success in the world could not have made the United States admirable so long as their spirit had this imperfection. Even if they had overrun the whole earth, their old national style would have still been detestable, and Mr. Beecher would have still been a heated barbarian. But they could not thus triumph, they could not make their rule thus universal, so long as their spirit was thus imperfect. They had not power enough over the minds of men. Now they are transforming their spirit in the furnace of civil war; with what success we shall in due time see. But the lovers of perfection in America itself ought to rejoice—some of them, no doubt, do rejoice—that the national spirit should be compelled, even at any cost of suffering, to transform itself, to become something higher, ampler, more gracious. To be glad that it should be compelled thus to transform itself, that it should not be permitted to triumph untransformed, is no insult, no unkindness; it is a homage to perfection. It is a religious devotion to that providential order which forbids the final supremacy of imperfect things. (God keeps tossing back to the human race its failures, and commanding it to try again.)

In the Crusade of Peter the Hermit, where the hosts that marched were not filled after the usual composition of armies, but contained along with the fighters whole families of people—old men, women, and children, swept by the universal torrent of enthusiasm towards the Holy Land —the marches, as might have been expected, were tedious and painful. Long before Asia was reached, long before even Europe was half traversed, the little children in that travelling multitude began to fancy, with a natural impatience, that their journey must surely be drawing to an end; and every evening, as they came in sight of some town which was the destination of that day's march, they cried out eagerly to those who were with them, "*Is this Jerusalem?*" No, poor children, not this town, nor the next, nor yet the next, is Jerusalem; Jerusalem is far off, and it needs time, and strength, and much endurance to reach it. Seas and mountains, labour and peril, hunger and thirst, disease and death, are between Jerusalem and you.

So, when one marks the ferment and stir of life in the middle class at this moment, and sees this class impelled to take possession of the world, and to assert itself and its own actual spirit absolutely, one is disposed to exclaim to it, "*Jerusalem is not yet.*" Your present spirit is not Jerusalem, is not the goal you have to reach, the place you may be satisfied in. And when one says this, they sometimes fancy that one has the same object as others who say the same to them; that one means that they are to yield themselves to be moulded by some existing force, their rival; that one wishes Nonconformity to take the law from actual Anglicanism, and the middle class from the present governing

H

class; that one thinks Anglicanism Jerusalem, and the English aristocratic class Jerusalem.

I do not mean, or wish, or think this, though many, no doubt, do. It is not easy for a reflecting man, who has studied its origin, to feel any vehement enthusiasm for Anglicanism; Henry the Eighth and his parliaments have taken care of that. One may esteem it as a beneficent social and civilising agent. One may have an affection for it from life-long associations, and for the sake of much that is venerable and interesting which it has inherited from antiquity. One may cherish gratitude to it— and here, I think, Mr. Goldwin Smith, who fights against it the battle of the Nonconformists with so much force and so much ability, is a little ungrateful—for the shelter and basis for culture which this, like other great nationally established forms of religion, affords; those who are born in them can get forward on their road, instead of always eyeing the ground on which they stand and disputing about it. But actual Anglicanism is certainly not Jerusalem, and I should be sorry to think it the end which Nonconformity and the middle class are to reach. The actual governing class, again, the English aristocratic class (in the widest sense of the word *aristocratic*)—I cannot wish that the rest of the nation, the new and growing part of the nation, should be transformed in spirit exactly according, to the image of that class. The merits and services of that class no one rates higher than I do; no one appreciates higher than I do the value of the relative standard of elevation, refinement and grandeur, which they have exhibited; no one would more strenuously oppose the relinquishing of this for any lower standard. But I cannot hide from myself that while modern societies increasingly tend to find their best life in a free and heightened spiritual and intellectual activity, to this tendency aristocracies offer at least a strong passive resistance, by their secular prejudices, their incurable dearth of ideas. In modern, rich, and industrial societies, they tend to misplace the ideal for the classes below them; the immaterial chivalrous ideal of high descent and honour is, by the very nature of the case, of force only for aristocracies themselves; the immaterial modern ideal of spiritual and intellectual perfection through culture, they have not to communicate. What they can and do communicate is the material ideal of splendour of wealth, and weight of property. And this ideal is the ideal truly operative upon our middle classes at this moment. To be as rich as they can, that they may reach the splendour of wealth and weight of property, and, with time, the importance, of the actual heads of society, is their ambition. I do not blame them, or the class from which they get their ideal; all I say is, that the good ideal for humanity, the true Jerusalem, is an ideal more spiritual than brilliant wealth and boundless property, an ideal in which more can participate. The beloved friends of humanity have been those who made it feel its ideal to be in the things of the mind and spirit, to be in an internal condition separable from wealth and accessible to all—men like St. Francis, the ardent bridegroom of poverty; men like the great personages of antiquity, almost all of them, as Lacordaire was so fond of saying, poor. Therefore, that the middle class should simply take its ideal from the aristocratic class, I do not wish. That the aristocratic class should be able absolutely to assert itself and its own spirit, is not my desire. No, no; they are not Jerusalem.

The truth is, the English spirit has to accomplish an immense evolution; nor, as that spirit at this moment presents itself in any class or description amongst us, can one be perfectly satisfied with it, can one wish it to prevail just as it is.

But in a transformed middle class, in a middle class raised to a higher and more genial culture, we may find, not perhaps Jerusalem, but, I am sure, a notable stage towards it. In that great class, strong by its numbers, its energy, its industry, strong by its freedom from frivolity, not by any law of nature prone to immobility of mind, actually at this moment agitated by a spreading ferment of mind, in that class, liberalised by an ampler culture, admitted to a wider sphere of thought, living by larger ideas, with its provincialism dissipated, its intolerance cured, its pettinesses purged away,—what a power there will be, what an element of new life for England! Then let the middle class rule, then let it affirm its own spirit, when it has thus perfected itself.

And I cannot see any means so direct and powerful for developing this great and beneficent power as the public establishment of schools for the middle class. By public establishment they may be made cheap and accessible to all. By public establishment they may give securities for the culture offered in them being really good and sound, and the best that our time knows. By public establishment they may communicate to those reared in them the sense of being brought in contact with their country, with the national life, with the life of the world; and they will expand and dignify their spirits by communicating this sense to them. I can see no other mode of institution which will offer the same advantages in the same degree.

I cannot think that the middle class will be much longer insensible to its own evident interests. I cannot think that, for the pleasure of being complimented on their self-reliance by Lord Fortescue and the *Times*, they will much longer forego a course leading them to their own true dignity instead of away from it. I know that with men who have reached or passed the middle of life, the language and habits of years form a network round the spirit through which it cannot easily break; and among the elder leaders of the middle class there are men whom I would give much to persuade—men of weight and character, like Mr. Baines, men of character and culture too, like Mr. Miall—whom I must not, I fear, hope to persuade. But among the younger leaders of this class—even of that part of it where resistance is most to be apprehended, among the younger Dissenting ministers, for instance—there exists, I do believe, a disposition not fixedly averse to the public establishment of education for the middle classes—a willingness, at any rate, to consider a project of this kind on its merits. Amongst them particularly is the ferment and expansion of mind, of which I have spoken, perceptible; their sense of the value of culture, and their culture itself, increases every day. Well, the old bugbear which scares us all away from the great confessed means of best promoting this culture—the religious difficulty, as it is called—is potent only so long as these gentlemen please. It rests solely with themselves to procure the public establishment of secondary instruction upon a perfectly equitable basis as regards religious differences. If its establishment is suffered to fix itself in private hands, those hands will be the clergy's. It is to the honour of the clergy—of their activity, of their corporate spirit, of their sense of a pressing want—that this should be so. But in that case the dominant force in settling the teaching in these schools will be clerical. Their organisation will be ecclesiastical. Mr. Woodard tells us so himself; and indeed he (very naturally) makes a merit of it.

This is not what the Dissenters want, neither is it what the movement of the modern spirit tends to. But when instruction has once been powerfully organised in this manner, it is very difficult for the State afterwards to interfere for the purpose of giving effect to the requirements of the modern spirit. It is met by vested interests—by legitimate vested interests—not to be conciliated without great delay and difficulty. It is not easy for the State to impose a conscience clause on primary schools, when the establishment of those schools has been for the most part made by the clergy. It is not easy to procure the full benefits of the national universities to Nonconformists, when Anglicanism has got a vested interest in the colleges. Neither will it be easy hereafter, in secondary instruction, to settle the religious difficulty equitably, if the establishment of that instruction shall have been effected by private bodies in which clerical influence predominates.

I hope the middle class will not much longer delay to take a step on which its future value and dignity and influence so much depend. By taking this step they will indirectly confer a great boon upon the lower class also. This obscure embryo, only just beginning to move, travailing in labour and darkness, so much left out of account when we celebrate the glories of our Atlantis, now and then, by so mournful a glimpse, showing itself to us in Lambeth, or Spitalfields, or Dorsetshire; this immense working class, now so without a practicable passage to all the joy and beauty of life, for whom in an aristocratic class, which is unattainable by them, there is no possible ideal, for whom in a middle class, narrow, ungenial, and unattractive, there is no adequate ideal, will have, in a cultured, liberalised, ennobled, transformed middle class, a point towards which it may hopefully work, a goal towards which it may with joy direct its aspirations.

Children of the future, whose day has not yet dawned, you, when that day arrives, will hardly believe what obstructions were long suffered to prevent its coming! You who, with all your faults, have neither the aridity of aristocracies, nor the narrow-mindedness of middle classes, you, whose power of simple enthusiasm is your great gift, will not comprehend how progress towards man's best perfection — the adorning and ennobling of his spirit—should have been reluctantly undertaken; how it should have been for years and years retarded by barren commonplaces, by worn-out clap-traps. You will wonder at the labour of its friends in proving the self-proving; you will know nothing of the doubts, the fears, the prejudices they had to dispel; nothing of the outcry they had to encounter; of the fierce protestations of life from policies which were dead and did not know it, and the shrill querulous upbraiding from publicists in their dotage. But you, in your turn, with difficulties of your own, will then be mounting some new step in the arduous ladder whereby man climbs towards his perfection; towards that unattainable but irresistible lode-star, gazed after with earnest longing, and invoked with bitter tears; the longing of thousands of hearts, the tears of many generations.

THE END.

www.ingramcontent.com/pod-product-compliance
Lightning Source LLC
Chambersburg PA
CBHW020127170426
43199CB00009B/670